Stars and Planets

Jacqueline Mitton

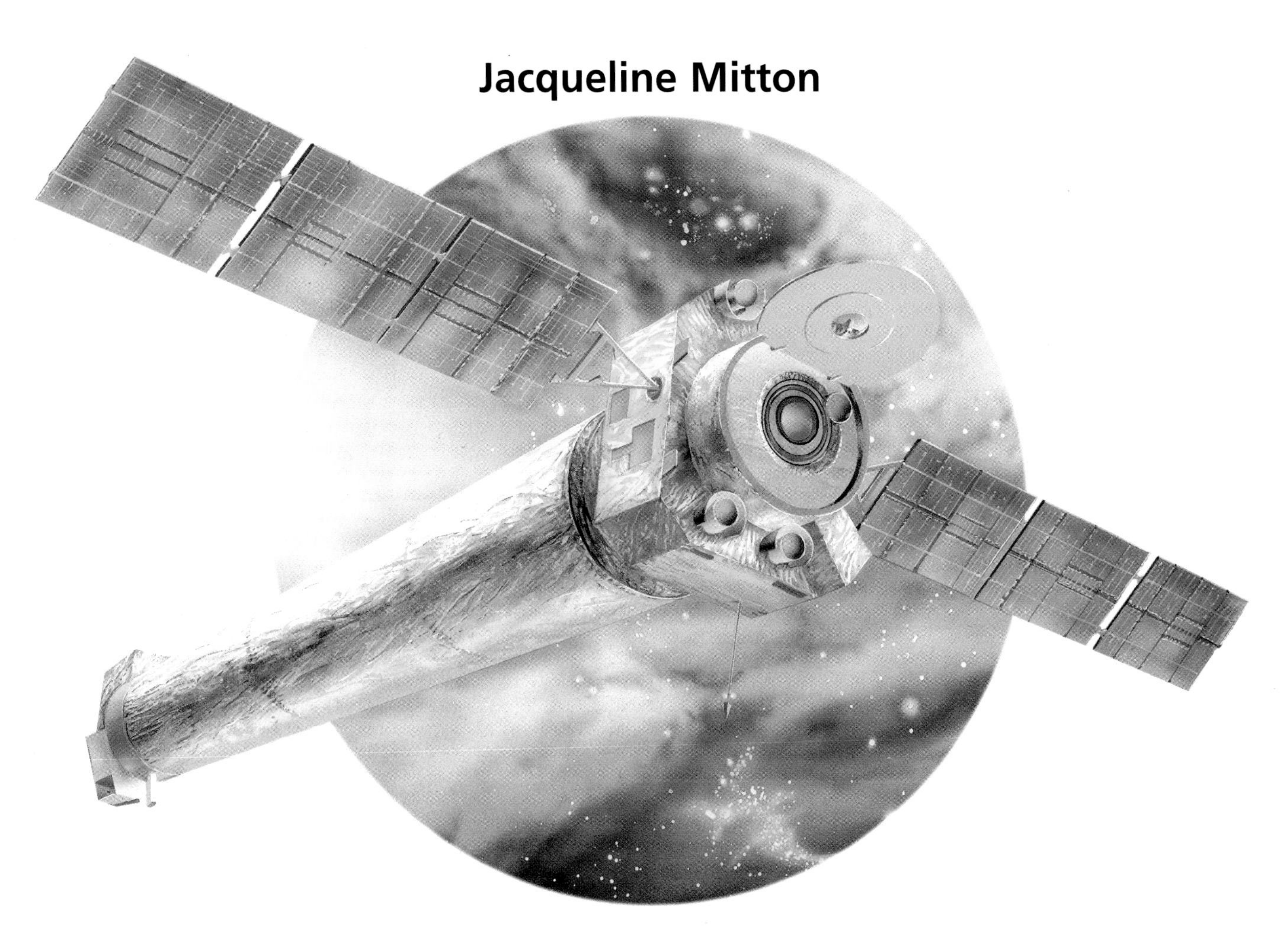

OXFORD
UNIVERSITY PRESS

OXFORD
UNIVERSITY PRESS

Great Clarendon Street, Oxford OX2 6DP

Oxford University Press is a department of the University of Oxford.
It furthers the University's objective of excellence in research, scholarship,
and education by publishing worldwide in

Oxford New York

Auckland Bangkok Buenos Aires Cape Town Chennai
Dar es Salaam Delhi Hong Kong Istanbul Karachi
Kolkata Kuala Lumpur Madrid Melbourne Mexico City Mumbai
Nairobi São Paulo Shanghai Singapore Taipei Tokyo Toronto

with an associated company in Berlin

Oxford is a registered trade mark of Oxford University Press
in the UK and in certain other countries

First published 2002

British Library Cataloguing in Publication Data available

Hardback ISBN 0-19-910709-2
Paperback ISBN 0-19-910710-6

1 3 5 7 9 10 8 6 4 2

Designed and typeset by Full Steam Ahead
Printed in Malaysia.

Contents

THE WONDERS OF THE UNIVERSE

On a clear moonless night, far from city lights, the starry sky is an awe-inspiring sight. You can see about 4000 stars when the sky is really dark. Astronomy is about far more than 'stars'. It is the science that aims to discover the secrets of the Universe.

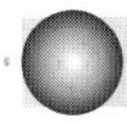

key words

- galaxy
- meteor
- planet
- radiation
- star

The Sun and all these stars belong to the huge star family we call the Milky Way Galaxy. Beyond our own galaxy, there are billions more in the Universe.

Some nights you might spot one or more of the bright planets, such as Venus or Jupiter. Like our own planet Earth, they belong to the Sun's family, called the Solar System. The planets are much nearer than the stars. They gradually move against the background of stars, which stays the same.

▲ The Lovell Telescope at Jodrell Bank in England is 76 metres across. It is one of the largest radio astronomy dishes in the world and can be pointed anywhere in the sky.

◀ An observatory at the Canada-France-Hawaii telescope on top of the Mauna Kea volcano, Hawaii. The dome-shaped building houses a large telescope. Its roof slides open and turns around. This picture was taken over a period of several hours. The trails of light in the sky are made by the stars. The stars slowly move round in the sky (like the Sun does during the day), because the Earth spins once a day.

Telescopes for astronomy

Spacecraft have been sent to explore the Moon and planets. However, most astronomy is done at observatories, with the help of telescopes and the electronic instruments that go on them.

The most familiar astronomical telescopes are optical ones, which pick up light from far-off objects. Astronomers also use special telescopes to detect invisible radiation from space, such as X-rays, infrared and radio waves.

They use the information they get from light and other kinds of radiation to find out how hot stars are, what gas clouds between stars are made of, and how fast the galaxies are moving away from us. They also find out many other facts about the Universe.

Large telescopes detect fainter objects and distinguish finer detail than smaller ones. The largest telescopes for optical and infrared astronomy have mirrors 8 or 10 metres across. The best places for these great observatories are remote mountain-tops where the air is clear and dry. Radio telescopes can pick up signals even through cloud, so they can be built almost anywhere. Some have large single dishes. Others use many smaller dishes that work together.

▶ You can discover lots of things about the night sky with the naked eye, or with the help of a small pair of binoculars.

Astronomy as a hobby

You don't have to be a professional scientist to do astronomy. You don't even need a telescope to start discovering the night sky. The first step is to learn some of the constellations. Next you can planet-spot and watch for meteors.

▼ Copernicus's plan of the Solar System.

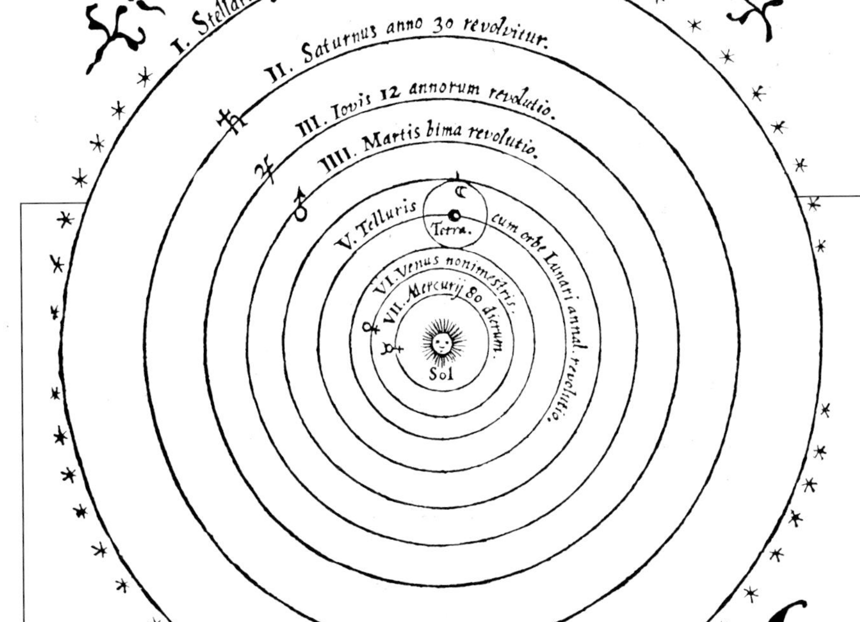

With a small telescope you can find many interesting sights, such as the rings around Saturn, but an ordinary pair of binoculars is a good start. They will show you the craters on the Moon, and clusters of stars in the Milky Way.

NICOLAUS COPERNICUS

Nicolaus Copernicus (1473–1543) was born in Poland. He was a student for many years, and was especially interested in astronomy. At that time most people believed that the Sun, the Moon and the planets all travelled around the Earth. Copernicus realized it is easier to explain the Solar System if the Sun is at the centre with the Earth and other planets orbiting around it.

OUT OF THIS WORLD

Space is a wonderful place for observing the stars. Above the Earth's atmosphere the sky is always dark and there are no clouds. The most exciting way to learn about other worlds in our Solar System is to send spacecraft to explore them in close-up.

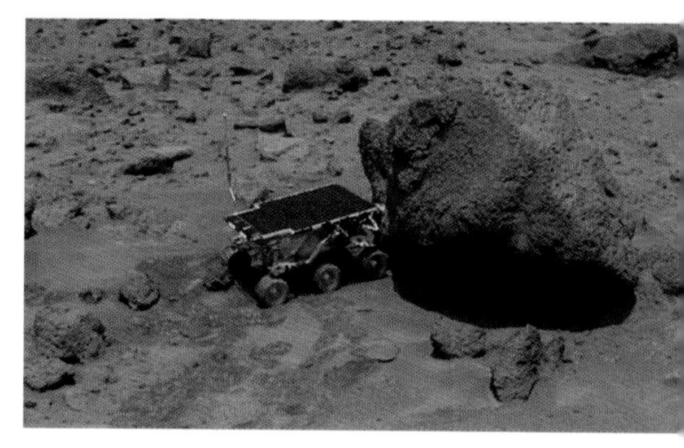

▲ This miniature rover was carried to Mars by the space probe *Mars Pathfinder*. In this slightly blurred image, relayed direct from Mars, it is studying a rock nicknamed 'Yogi'.

For astronomers, the atmosphere is a nuisance. From the Earth, stars never look truly sharp because the air makes them twinkle. Even worse, the air absorbs invisible kinds of radiation such as X-rays, ultraviolet rays and infrared rays. These kinds of radiation can give astronomers valuable extra information about planets, stars and galaxies.

▶ This picture of the sky shows the remains of an exploded star, known as the Crab Nebula. It was taken by the Chandra X-ray Observatory.

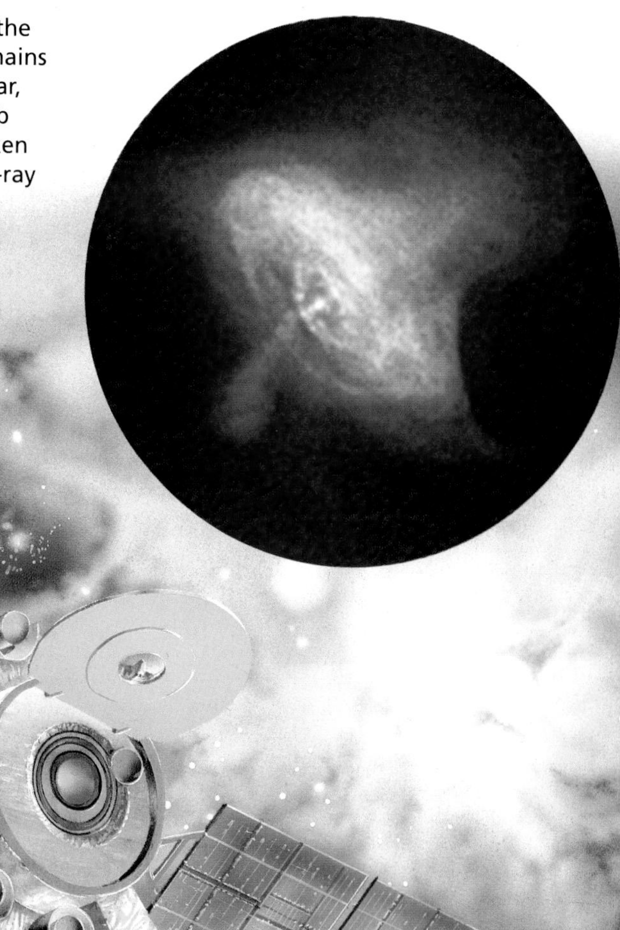

▶ The Chandra X-ray Observatory was launched into an orbit thousands of kilometres above the Earth by the space shuttle *Columbia* in July 1999.

THE HUBBLE SPACE TELESCOPE

The space shuttle *Discovery* carried the Hubble Space Telescope into orbit in April 1990. It circles the Earth every 90 minutes, about 600 kilometres above us.

The telescope's main mirror is 2.4 metres across. It is used to observe ultraviolet and infrared rays as well as visible light. The telescope beams its observations back to Earth as radio signals. The two 'paddles' on either side of the tube are solar panels. They convert sunlight into electrical power. Astronauts have travelled to the telescope on board the space shuttle several times to make repairs and change old instruments for more modern ones.

key words

- atmosphere
- infrared radiation
- ultraviolet
- X-rays

Satellites in space

To overcome these problems, many astronomy satellites have been put into orbit around the Earth since the 1960s. Some satellites are launched on rockets. Others are taken on board a space shuttle. Successful ones usually work for several years. These satellites carry special telescopes that are built to pick up each different kind of radiation.

Exploring the Solar System

Every planet in the Solar System, apart from Pluto, has been visited by a spacecraft at least once. There have also been missions to asteroids and comets, and to our own Moon. These interplanetary explorers carry television cameras which beam images back to Earth, and instruments to measure such things as a planet's magnetic field.

Sometimes spacecraft just fly past their targets, returning information for only a few hours. The most successful flyby mission ever was *Voyager* 2, launched in 1977. It toured all four giant planets: Jupiter, Saturn, Uranus and Neptune.

Orbiters, probes and landers

A spacecraft orbiting a planet or moon – called an 'orbiter' – sometimes stays in service for years. The two *Lunar Orbiter* spacecraft, sent to the Moon in 1966 and 1967, made maps of the Moon to prepare for later manned landings. *Mars Global Surveyor* began to make detailed maps of the whole of Mars in 1999.

Galileo was put into orbit around Jupiter at the end of 1995 and stayed there for several years. It released a probe that went down into Jupiter's atmosphere. Venus has also been studied by atmosphere probes, such as *Pioneer Venus* 2, launched in 1978.

Some spacecraft are designed to land softly on a planet's surface. Sometimes landers are released by orbiters, which continue to circle overhead. The two *Viking* space probes, which reached Mars in 1976, released landers that tested the soil for signs of life. These landers also sent back the first pictures from the surface of Mars.

▼ The *Cassini* spacecraft will release a probe when it arrives to orbit Saturn in 2004. The probe will parachute down through the hazy atmosphere of Saturn's largest moon, Titan. Its six instruments will beam back pictures and data.

THE STARRY SKY

Look up at the starry sky and you will soon notice how the bright stars make shapes. There are lines, squares, crosses and a letter 'W' and a cross. Seeing patterns in the stars and giving them names goes back thousands of years.

The patterns in the stars are called constellations. Through history, different civilizations have had their own constellations. People making new star maps have made changes to the constellations and invented new ones. In 1930, astronomers finally agreed how to divide the whole sky into 88 areas, which are now the official constellations. Forty-eight of them date back to the 2nd century AD.

The constellations you can see depend on your latitude on the Earth. If you live in the northern hemisphere, there are constellations you will never see unless you travel to the southern hemisphere – and the other way round. Most of the southern constellations were named by travellers in the 16th and 17th centuries.

Many of the brighter stars also have traditional names of their own. They are usually Latin or Arabic words.

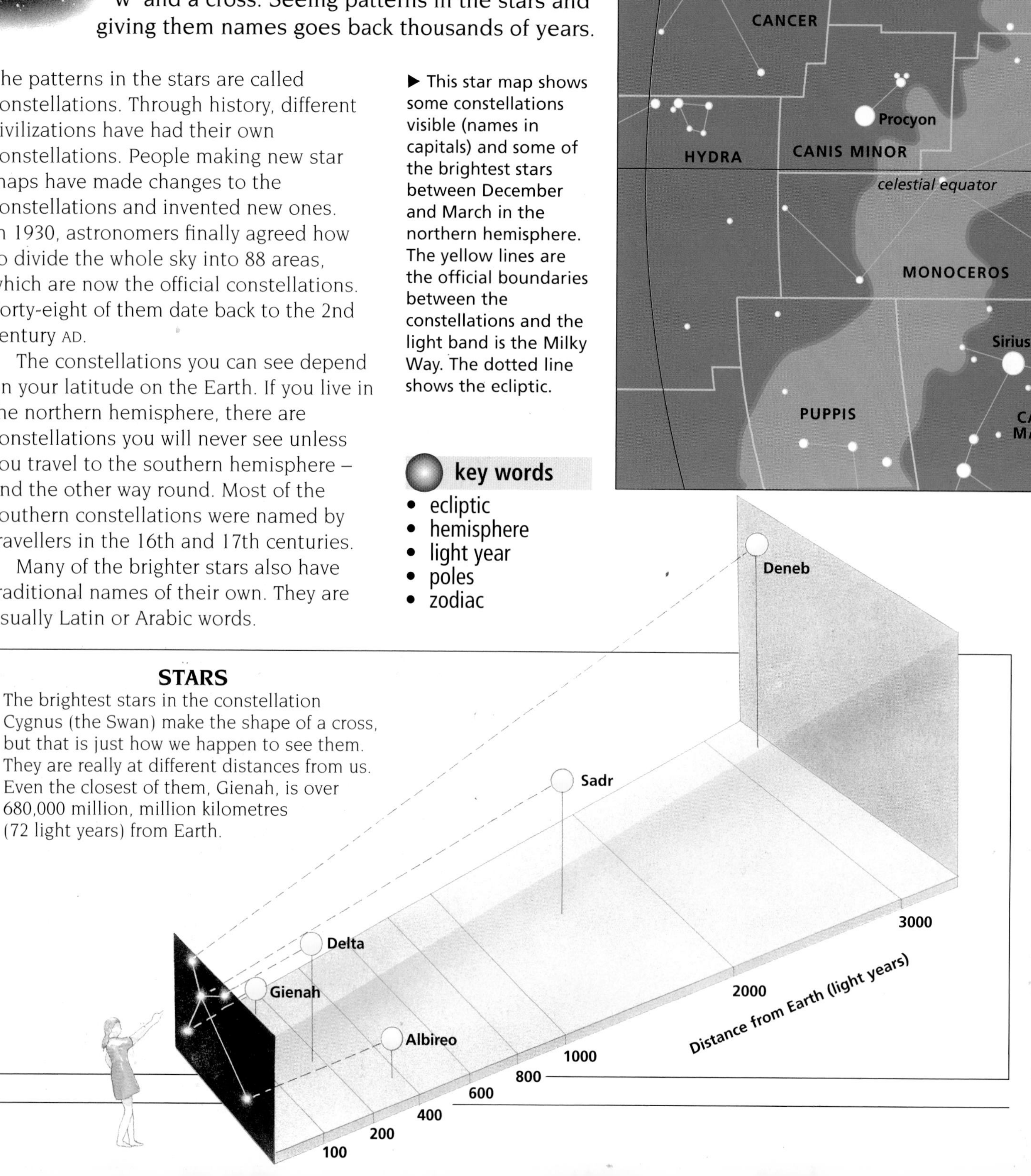

▶ This star map shows some constellations visible (names in capitals) and some of the brightest stars between December and March in the northern hemisphere. The yellow lines are the official boundaries between the constellations and the light band is the Milky Way. The dotted line shows the ecliptic.

key words

- ecliptic
- hemisphere
- light year
- poles
- zodiac

STARS

The brightest stars in the constellation Cygnus (the Swan) make the shape of a cross, but that is just how we happen to see them. They are really at different distances from us. Even the closest of them, Gienah, is over 680,000 million, million kilometres (72 light years) from Earth.

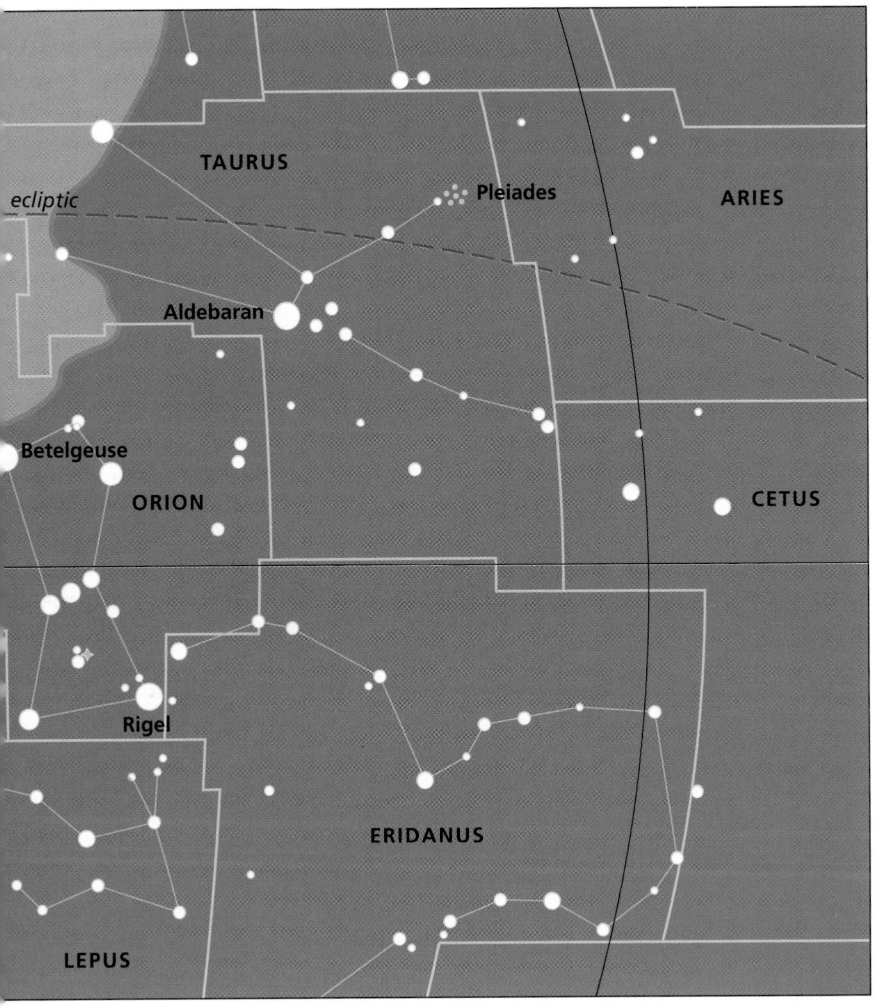

The Sun and the zodiac

If the stars were visible during the day, we would see that the Sun gradually moves through the constellations. Over a year, it covers a complete circle, called the ecliptic. The planets are always near to the ecliptic too.

The ecliptic goes through the 12 constellations traditionally called the zodiac: Aries, Taurus, Gemini, Cancer, Leo, Virgo, Libra, Scorpius, Sagittarius, Capricornus, Aquarius and Pisces. Astrologers divide the zodiac band into 12 equal parts, called 'signs', with the same names, but these do not coincide with the astronomical constellations.

The stars are so far away that their distances are often given in light years instead of kilometres. A light year is the distance light travels in one year. The speed of light is nearly 300,000 kilometres per second. In a year light travels 9461 million million kilometres.

▼ The constellations of the zodiac and how the Sun moves around the ecliptic through the year.

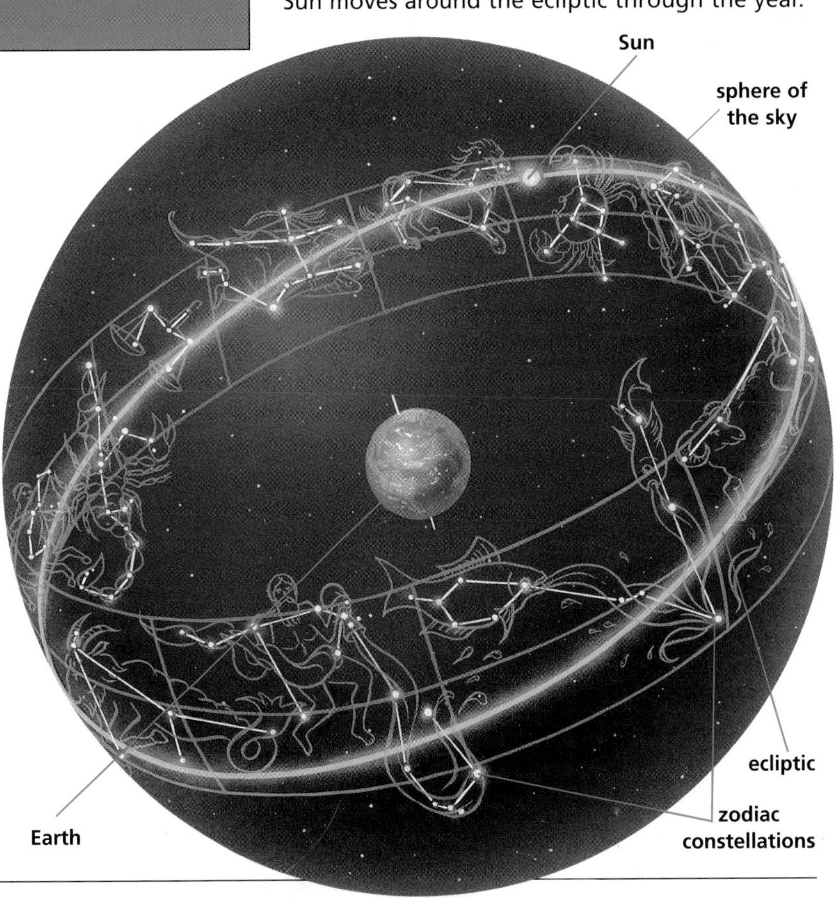

The sphere of the sky

The stars in a constellation look as though they are close together, but in actual fact they are scattered through space at different distances from us. It is simply that we cannot tell that just by looking up at the sky.

At any particular time, half of the stars visible in space are hidden below our horizon. But we see a sequence of different constellations through the night, because the Earth is turning.

The whole sky seems to revolve about its North and South Poles. In the same way that the Sun rises and sets each day, stars also rise in the east and set in the west. Some constellations near the poles never set, though. They circle around the sky without ever sinking below the horizon.

The constellations visible when it is dark also change gradually through the seasons. This happens because the stars rise 4 minutes earlier every day.

THE SUN'S FAMILY

Nine major planets travel around the Sun, kept in their orbits by the Sun's strong gravity. They are the chief members of the Solar System. Moons circle around seven of them and there are more than 60 moons altogether. The Sun's family also includes many thousands of small objects – asteroids, comets and meteoroids.

The orbits of the planets from Mercury nearest the Sun, out to Neptune, are arranged in space almost in a flat disc, like hoops lying on a table. The paths the planets follow are not circles, though, but ellipses – slightly squashed circles. Pluto is the odd planet out. Its orbit is tilted to the others and is much more stretched out into a long elliptical shape.

Pluto's strange orbit was a mystery. Then in the 1990s, astronomers discovered that Pluto was not the only world beyond Neptune. They found dozens of miniature icy planets orbiting in a doughnut-shaped belt. There are probably thousands of them altogether. So far, none has been found any larger than Pluto.

▶ A great shell of comets called the Oort Cloud marks the most remote edge of the Solar System.

key words

- ellipse
- gravity
- orbit

KEPLER AND MOVEMENT OF THE PLANETS

Johannes Kepler (1571–1630) was a German astronomer who studied the motion of Mars. He worked out for the first time that the planets follow elliptical orbits rather than circular ones. He also discovered other rules about how they move.

As it travels around its elliptical orbit, a planet's distance from the Sun varies. Kepler found out that a planet moves more quickly when it is nearer the Sun. He also explained how planets farther from the Sun take longer to complete their orbit than those that are closer.

Asteroids and meteoroids

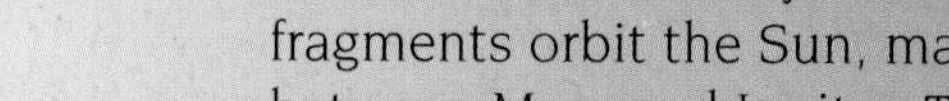

Nearer the Sun, many thousands of rocky fragments orbit the Sun, mainly in a belt between Mars and Jupiter. These are the asteroids, sometimes called minor planets.

Some chunks of rock between the planets are too small even to count as asteroids. They range from large boulders to dust-like bits and pieces. These are called meteoroids. Even the smallest follow their own paths in orbit around the Sun.

The most remote members of the Solar System are comets. Millions of them swarm in a ball-shaped cloud 2000 to 20,000 times further from the Sun than the Earth. At this great distance comets are too faint to be seen. We only see the few comets that come in close to the Earth.

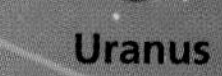

▲▶ In this illustration of the Solar System, the orbits of the planets are shown approximately to scale. However, the Sun and the planets themselves are shown much larger – at this scale they would actually be smaller than pinpricks.

IN THE BEGINNING

The history of the Solar System goes back about 4600 million years. When the Sun first formed, it was spinning slowly. A huge disc of gas and dust spread out around its middle (a). Material began to clump together in the disc. Some of the small clumps merged into bigger ones. Sometimes they collided so hard that they broke up again (b).

After millions of years, the largest clumps had become the planets (c). Comets and asteroids are the smaller, leftover pieces. Over time they settled in the zones where they are today. Comets are the most remote members of the Solar System. There are millions of them in a region up to 20,000 times farther from the Sun than the Earth – even farther away than Pluto.

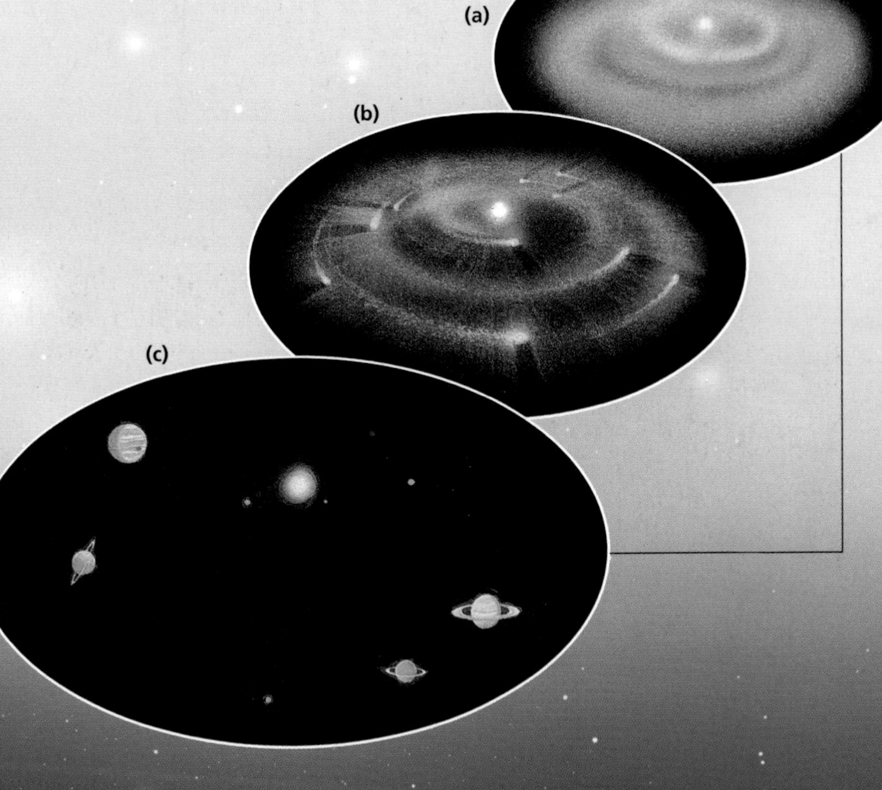

Mars Mercury Sun Venus

Saturn

Earth Jupiter

THE ORBITS OF THE PLANETS

Planet	Average distance from Sun (million km)	Time taken to orbit Sun (to nearest Earth day/year)
Mercury	58	88 days
Venus	108	225 days
Earth	150	365 days
Mars	228	687 days
Jupiter	778	12 years
Saturn	1427	30 years
Uranus	2860	84 years
Neptune	4500	165 years
Pluto	4435 (nearest), 7372 (farthest)	248 years

Our nearest star

Shining bright and yellow in the daytime sky, the Sun gives us light and warmth. Most life on Earth needs energy from the Sun to grow and to survive.

The Sun is our very own star – a gigantic ball of glowing gas. It is like the stars that we see in night sky, but much nearer. Among the stars, our Sun is middle-sized and nothing out of the ordinary. But for plants and animals on Earth the Sun is very special. Plants use the energy in sunlight to grow. This process is called photosynthesis. The warmth from the Sun makes our planet a good home for all kinds of living things.

The Sun is mostly made of hydrogen. Like all stars, it generates nuclear energy at its centre. In the process, hydrogen changes to helium – the gas used to fill party balloons. As the hydrogen is turned into helium the Sun gets lighter in weight losing 4 million tonnes every second. The Sun is not about to run out of hydrogen fuel, though. It has been shining for 5000 million years already and will last for around 5000 million more.

▶ The Sun's appearance is constantly changing. The dark patches are sunspots, which last no longer than a few weeks. Sunspots look dark because they are about 1500°C cooler than the surrounding areas.

SUN FACTS
Diameter: 1.4 million km
Mass: 333,000 times Earth's mass
Temperature (surface): 5500 °C
(centre): 15 million °C
Average distance from Earth: 150 million km

A seething surface

The visible yellow surface of the Sun is called the photosphere. It seems to bubble like a cauldron as hot gas surges up and falls back again. The photosphere is surrounded by the Sun's atmosphere. It is made of thin, very hot gas that we do not normally see.

key words

- corona
- hydrogen
- magnetism
- nuclear energy
- solar wind

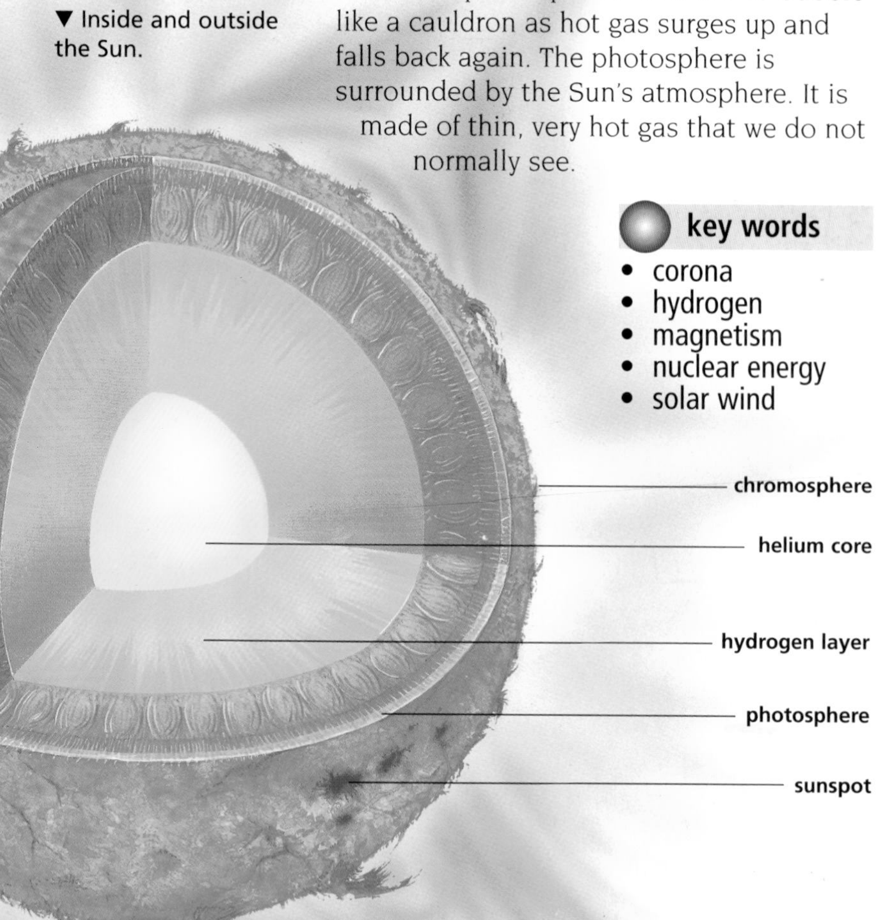

▼ Inside and outside the Sun.

Just above the photosphere there is a layer of gas about 5000 kilometres thick called the chromosphere. Sometimes, huge flares explode in the chromosphere. They blast gas particles far into space, even as far as the Earth and beyond. These solar flares can interfere with radio communications on Earth, and are dangerous for astronauts working in space.

The chromosphere merges into the corona, which is the outermost part of the Sun. Temperatures in the corona can be as high as 3 million °C. The corona can be seen when the bright photosphere is hidden by the Moon during a total eclipse. It extends millions of kilometres into space.

▼ A false-colour close-up of a sunspot, taken by the Dutch Open Telescope. These shallow pits on the Sun can be larger than the Earth. Around this sunspot you can see the pattern of the Sun's surface, caused by bubbling gas.

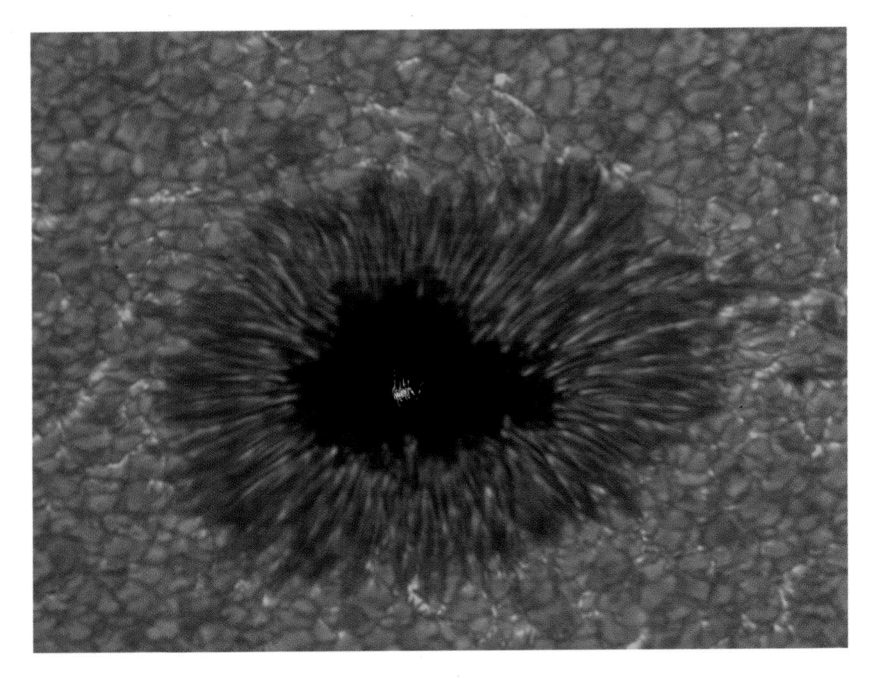

Tiny particles are constantly streaming away from the corona towards the planets, creating a solar wind. The solar wind blows past the Earth at speeds of up to 800 kilometres per second.

The Sun's magnetism

Sunspots are dark, slightly cooler patches on the surface of the Sun. When and where sunspots appear is linked to the Sun's magnetism. Astronomers have noticed that the appearance and disappearance of sunspots follows a regular cycle. Sunspot activity reaches a maximum every 11 years, then falls off. Regular changes in the Sun's magnetic field tie in with this 11-year cycle.

WARNING!
Do not look at the Sun, even through sunglasses. Without special equipment you could permanently damage your eyesight.

THE SUN'S MAGNETIC CYCLE

Changes in the Sun's magnetic field happen in a regular cycle of 11 years.

At the start of the cycle (a), lines of magnetic force run north and south between the Sun's poles. At this time there is minimum solar activity.

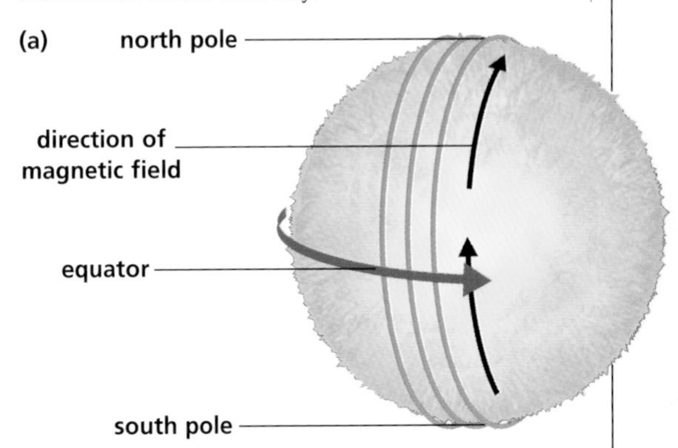

As the Sun rotates, the atmosphere spins faster at the equator than it does at Poles. The lines of magnetic force between the poles begin to bend (b).

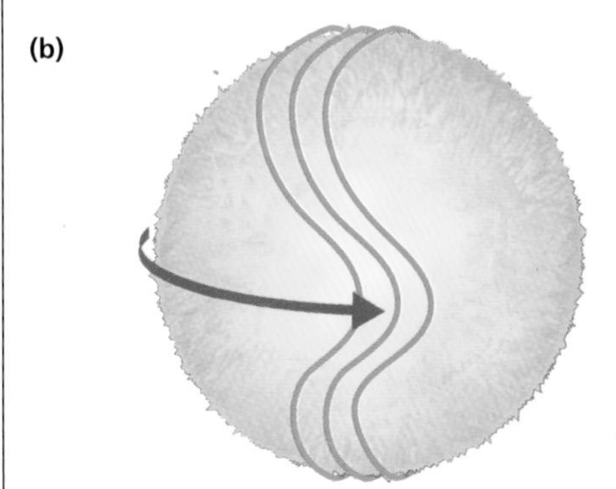

As time goes on, the magnetic field bends more and more. The effect is rather like an elastic band stretching (c).

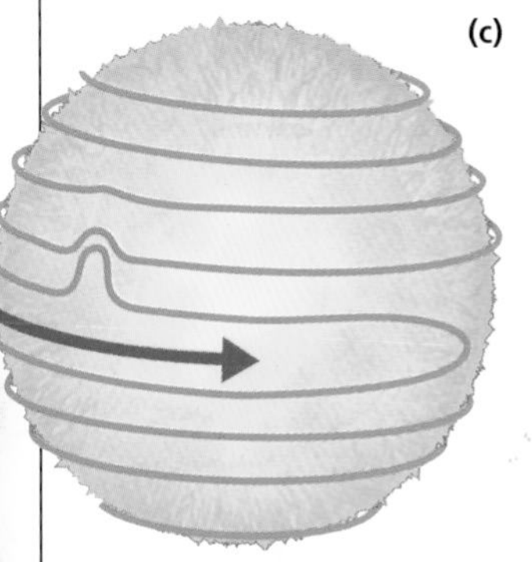

When the magnetic field cannot bend any further, it snaps and twists. This releases energy, causing violent activity to erupt on the Sun. After this maximum, the cycle begins again.

EARTH'S PARTNER

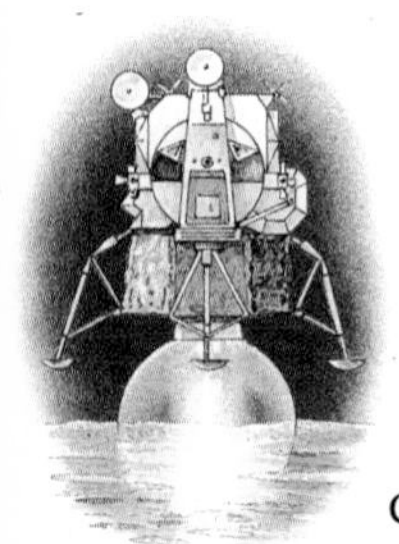

On 20 July 1969, astronauts Neil Armstrong and Buzz Aldrin landed on the Moon and became the first people ever to go there. They found themselves on a bleak lifeless world with crunchy grey soil under their feet. The Sun shone from a completely black sky overhead.

▲ Astronaut James Irwin with the lunar rover during the *Apollo 15* mission to the Moon. The lunar rover was used on the later Moon missions to explore large areas around the landing site.

The Moon is planet Earth's natural satellite. Other planets have moons that orbit them, too. Our Moon is a barren ball of rock about one quarter the diameter of the Earth. It has no atmosphere, no liquid water and no life. Hardly anything has changed on the Moon for thousands of millions of years.

Even without a telescope, you can see dark and bright areas. The dark regions formed when molten rock welled up into great basins on the surface thousands of millions of years ago. They were named *maria* (Latin for 'seas') on early maps of the Moon, but they are really rocky plains. The first astronauts to land touched down on the Sea of Tranquillity. The lighter parts of the Moon's surface are mountainous highland areas.

key words

- crater
- phases
- satellite

Craters everywhere

The Moon is littered with craters. They were gouged out by rocks crashing down from space. Most were made soon after the Moon formed. Larger rocks called asteroids

MOON DATA
Diameter: 3476 km
Average distance from Earth: 384,400 km
Mass: 0.012 Earth's mass
Time taken to orbit the Earth: 27.33 days
Time taken to spin on axis: 27.33 days
Time between new Moons: 29.53 days

◀ This photo of the Moon's surface shows a large crater.

produced the basins that later became the 'seas'. There are fewer craters on the 'sea' areas than in the highlands.

Crater sizes range from a few centimetres up to about 100 kilometres. A few are even wider. The largest crater on the Moon is called Bailly and is 295 kilometres across.

Near and far

The Moon orbits the Earth at a distance of about 385,000 kilometres. The Moon's gravity is less than a fifth of the Earth's, but because it is so close, its gravitational pull is the main cause of the Earth's tides. The Moon takes the same time to orbit the Earth as it does to spin once on its axis. This means the same side of the Moon, known as its near side, always faces the Earth. Spacecraft have returned images of the Moon's far side. It has many craters but far fewer 'sea' areas.

How the Earth got its Moon

Astronomers have long puzzled about where the Moon came from. The most popular idea is that a large asteroid crashed into the Earth very soon after it first formed. The huge impact spewed vast amounts of rock into space. Some of it circled around the Earth. Then the pull of gravity caused some of the rock fragments to come together and form the Moon.

THE MOON'S PHASES

Sunlight makes the side of the Moon facing the Sun shine. On this part of the Moon it is daytime. The other half is in darkness and here it is night. As the Moon travels around the Earth, we see different amounts of its sunlit half. Night by night, the shape of the Moon seems to change from a thin crescent to a complete disc and back again. The shape of the Moon is called its phase.

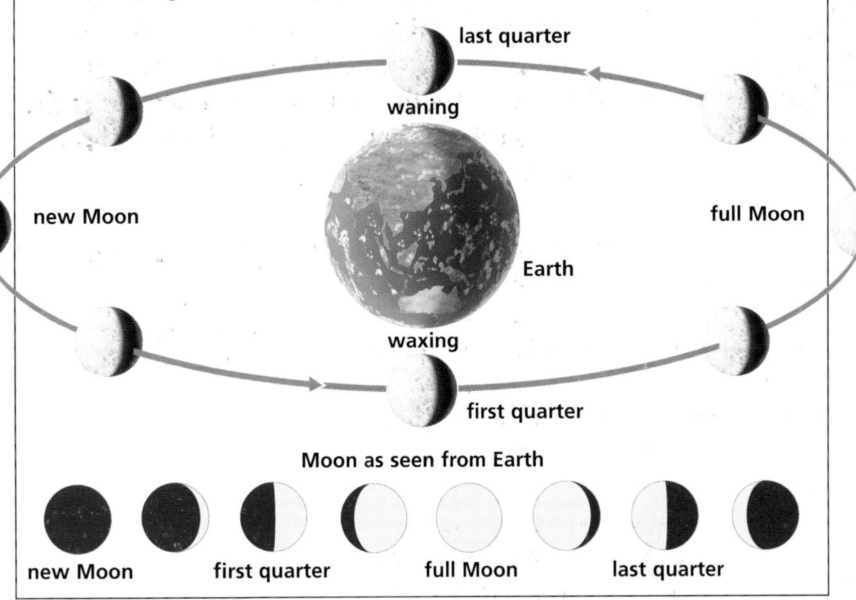

The Apollo missions

Six crews of American astronauts made successful Moon landings between July 1969 and December 1972. The commander of each mission remained in orbit round the Moon, while the lunar module undocked and took two astronauts down to the surface.

When the astronauts had finished working on the surface, the lunar module launched them back into orbit. They rejoined the command and service modules, which carried all three astronauts back to Earth.

The Apollo astronauts collected 400 kilograms of Moon rocks in all and carried out a variety of experiments. The last three crews took an electric powered Lunar Rover, or Moon buggy, to ride in so they could explore farther afield.

▶ A map of the Moon showing the names of some of the main features. The easiest crater to spot is Tycho. It is 85 km across and has a mountain peak in the centre.

SHADOWS IN SPACE

Only a narrow crescent of Sun is visible and the sky is darkening rapidly. Suddenly, the last bead of sunlight disappears behind the Moon. A thin ring of pink fire and a halo of pearly light surround the dark disc of the Moon. A total eclipse of the Sun has reached its climax.

When the Moon passes between the Earth and the Sun, it can just cover the Sun's dazzling yellow disc. Then the faint outer part of the Sun, called the corona, becomes visible. We can see this awe-inspiring sight because of an amazing coincidence: the Moon and the Sun appear nearly the same size. In reality, the Sun is 400 times larger than the Moon, but it is also 400 times farther away.

Totality is the time while the Sun's yellow disc is completely covered. It can last several minutes. This can only be seen where the Moon's deepest shadow sweeps across the Earth's surface. Over a larger region there is a partial eclipse, which means that the Sun is partly covered by the Moon. During a partial eclipse the sky does not get dark and the corona is not visible. There can be partial solar eclipses when nowhere has totality.

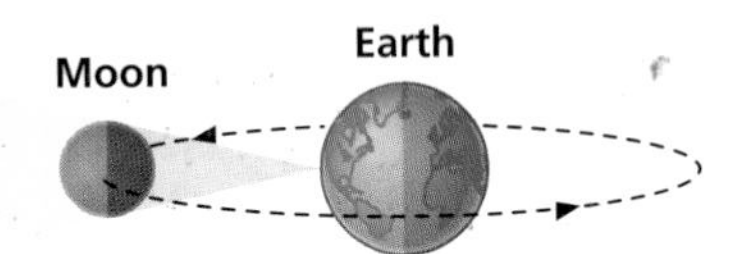

SOLAR ECLIPSE

▲ Totality during an eclipse of the Sun. Solar eclipses happen at New Moon when the Moon passes between the Earth and the Sun. The Sun's corona is visible as long as the bright disc of the Sun is covered by the Moon.

key words

- atmosphere
- corona
- eclipse
- shadow
- totality

▼ Lunar eclipses take place at Full Moon, when the Moon moves into the Earth's shadow. The Moon looks orange during a total lunar eclipse.

Sun

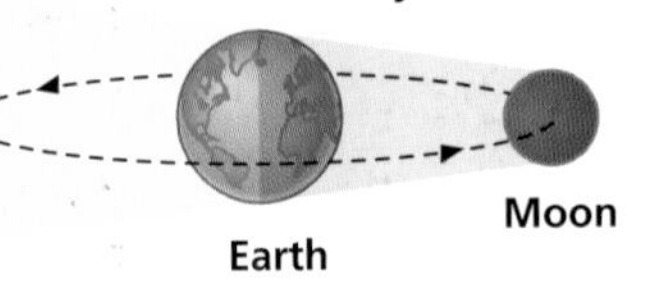

LUNAR ECLIPSE

Lunar eclipses

The Moon sometimes passes into the Earth's shadow. Nearly all sunlight to the Moon is cut off and there is a lunar eclipse. The Moon does not vanish from sight, though. It usually looks a dim orange-brown colour. It is lit by sunlight spilt into the Earth's shadow by the atmosphere. Lunar eclipses are visible from all places on the Earth where the Moon is up and can last as long as 2.5 hours.

OTHER WORLDS

On a clear night you may spot a planet shining brightly – perhaps Venus, Jupiter or even Mars. The planets do not give out any light of their own. They shine because they reflect the light of the Sun.

To ancient astronomers, the planets were all the heavenly bodies that moved around in the sky while the stars stayed in the same places. 'Planet' comes from a Greek word meaning 'wanderer'. Today astronomers use the word 'planet' to mean a world in orbit around a star.

Our Solar System has nine major planets orbiting the Sun. They are Mercury, Venus, Earth, Mars, Jupiter, Saturn, Uranus, Neptune and Pluto. They all travel around the Sun in the same direction and all spin on their axes, but apart from that they are a strange assortment. Jupiter is 60 times larger than Pluto. Four are rocky, four mostly gas and liquid, and one icy.

▲ There is evidence that many other stars also have planets around them. One of the first to be discovered was a large planet orbiting the star Tau Boötis. This artist's impression of the planet shows it with a moon, although astronomers do not yet know if it has one.

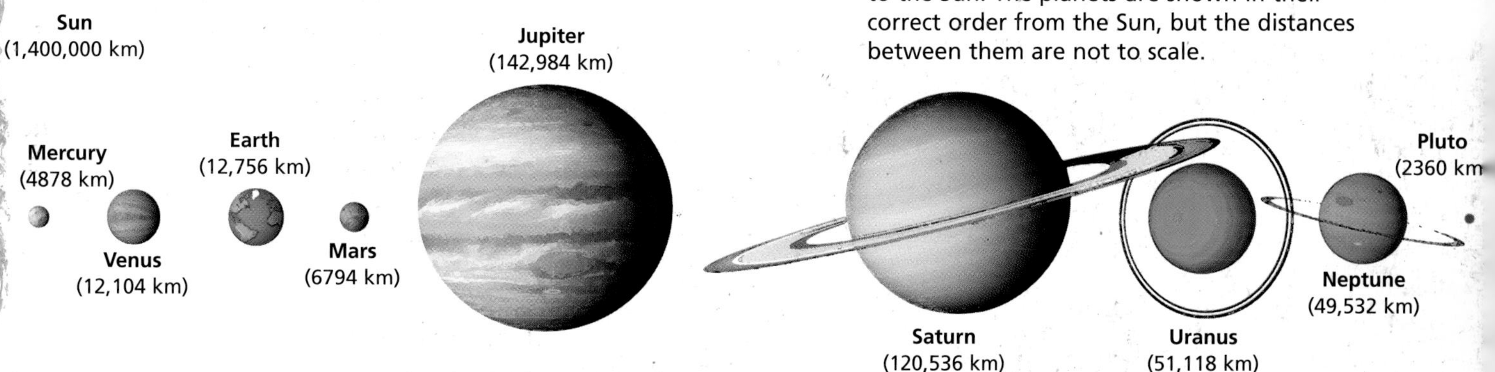

▼ A comparison of the sizes of the planets (their diameters) of our own Solar System in relation to the Sun. The planets are shown in their correct order from the Sun, but the distances between them are not to scale.

Different kinds of planets

In the Solar System, there are three other planets that are rocky like Earth: Mercury, Venus and Mars. They are sometimes called the terrestrial planets. The four giant planets – Jupiter, Saturn, Uranus and Neptune – are completely different. They have small rocky cores but are covered by deep layers of liquid and gas.

Pluto is different again. It is made of a mixture of ice and rock, and is by far the smallest planet. Pluto is more like some of the large moons orbiting the giant planets. These large moons are really no different from planets, but they happen to go round a planet rather than the Sun. Jupiter's moon Ganymede and Saturn's moon Titan are both larger than Mercury.

key words
- moon
- orbit
- planet
- rocky planets

A SCORCHED PLANET

A huge Sun beats down from Mercury's sky. Its fierce heat bakes the rocky surface and the temperature soars to 450 °C, hot enough to melt lead. But when the Sun goes down a big chill sets in on the planet closest to the Sun.

Temperature swings on Mercury are greater than those on any other planet. With no atmosphere to hold in the heat, the surface cools down to –180 °C at night. There could even be ice near Mercury's poles, shaded from the Sun inside deep craters.

Mercury spins very slowly while speeding around the Sun. This has a strange effect. In the time between one sunrise and the next, Mercury completes two orbits. That takes 176 Earth days, so days and nights are very long, which is why the temperatures are so extreme.

▶ The only close-up pictures of Mercury were taken by the spacecraft *Mariner 10*, which flew past three times in 1974–1975. This illustration is based on the Mariner photos.

MERCURY DATA
Diameter at equator: 4878 km
Average distance from Sun: 57.9 million km
Time taken to spin on axis: 58.6 days
Density (water = 1): 5.4
Time taken to orbit the Sun: 88.0 days
Moons: 0

Hide and seek

Mercury is difficult to observe. Though bright, it is always near the Sun and mostly hidden in the glare. But every few weeks it dodges out far enough to be spotted for a few days at dusk or dawn. Through a telescope, Mercury usually looks like a half-moon or crescent. We see these different shapes, or phases, because Mercury is closer to the Sun than us.

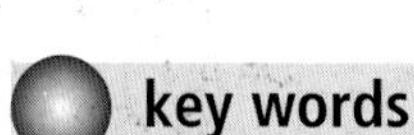

key words

- craters
- orbit
- phases
- planet

◀ This is a close-up of the surface of Mercury returned by *Mariner 10*, showing part of the Caloris Basin on the left.

A battered surface

Mercury's surface is peppered all over with thousands of craters where meteorites once rained down. One enormous impact by a rock about 100 kilometres across created the Caloris Basin. Surrounded by several rings of mountains and partly filled in, it is 1300 kilometres wide.

Long ridges cross the surface with cliffs up to 3000 metres high. They formed over 3000 million years ago when Mercury shrank as it cooled down.

Mercury's surface rocky layer is much thinner than Earth's. Beneath it is a huge iron core, about 1900 kilometres across.

THE VEILED PLANET

The most brilliant planet in the sky, Venus is our closest planet. You may spot it in the western sky after sunset or in the east before sunrise. Yet no one has ever seen its surface. Acid clouds completely conceal this forbidding world.

Venus is a rocky planet almost the same size as the Earth but it is very different. An atmosphere nearly 100 times thicker than the Earth's presses down on Venus. It is almost all carbon dioxide, a gas that easily traps the heat of the Sun. Fifty kilometres above the ground, droplets of sulphuric acid form dense clouds that never clear away.

On the planet's surface, the temperature reaches 480 °C – hotter even than Mercury. And there is hardly any difference between day and night. Venus is a sweltering, hostile place.

Though it is impossible to see through Venus's clouds, radio waves can get through. So astronomers have used radar to map the hidden surface.

key words

- clouds
- planet
- radar
- volcanoes

Volcanoes and craters

Venus has thousands of volcanoes. Volcanic activity may even be going on right now, as it is on Earth. Typical volcanoes are about 3 kilometres across and 90 metres high, but some are much larger. Gula Mons, for example, is 3 kilometres high.

Lava channels snake for thousands of kilometres and Venus has some volcanic features seen on no other planets. Some are like spiders with ridges radiating outwards. There are flat-topped volcanoes up to 60 kilometres across, which are called 'pancake domes'.

There are about 900 craters on Venus. The largest are 250 kilometres across. Even the smallest are about 1.5 kilometres. This is because only larger rocks can get through the atmosphere without burning up.

VENUS DATA
Diameter at equator: 12,104 km
Average distance from Sun: 108 million km
Time taken to spin on axis: 243 days (backwards)
Density (water = 1): 5.2
Time taken to orbit the Sun: 224.68 days
Moons: 0

▲ What Venus's volcanic landscape might look like.

◄ ▼ A picture of Venus (left), taken by the Pioneer Space Telescope, shows the planet covered with clouds. A radar map (below) reveals the surface underneath. The lighter band is one of the two major highland areas.

HAVEN OF LIFE

The third planet from the Sun is the largest rocky planet. It has craters like Mercury, volcanoes like Venus and polar caps like Mars. But unlike any other planet the Earth has oceans and over a million different kinds of living things.

Viewed from space, Earth is a beautiful blue planet. About 70 per cent of its surface is submerged under liquid water that is 4 kilometres deep on average. Frozen water covers about 10 per cent of the Earth, mostly at the North and South Poles. White clouds swirling in the atmosphere are droplets formed from the water vapour in the air.

No other planet in the Solar System has just the right range of temperature and a thick enough atmosphere for water to be liquid on the surface. And it is the water that makes the Earth a home for life.

key words

- atmosphere
- continents
- life
- planet
- water

Moving through space

The Earth is constantly moving through space, travelling around the Sun at a distance of about 150 million kilometres. The complete journey takes a year – just over 365 days. As it orbits, the Earth spins on its own axis, once each day. Its axis is tilted over at an angle of 23.5 degrees.

The life zone

If the Earth were much nearer the Sun or much farther away, it would be too hot or too cold for water and life. As it is, with the help of the atmosphere to keep warmth in and even out the climate, the Earth is just right. The atmosphere is important. Today

EARTH DATA
Diameter at equator: 12,756 km
Average distance from Sun: 150 million km
Time taken to spin on axis: 24 hours (relative to Sun)
Density (water = 1): 5.5
Time taken to orbit the Sun: 1 year
Moons: 1

▲ At night, the lights on Earth from human habitation can be seen from way out in space.

◀ Earth from space, showing clouds cover the continent of South America. This view was taken from space by the *Galileo* spacecraft when it was about 2.5 million kilometres away.

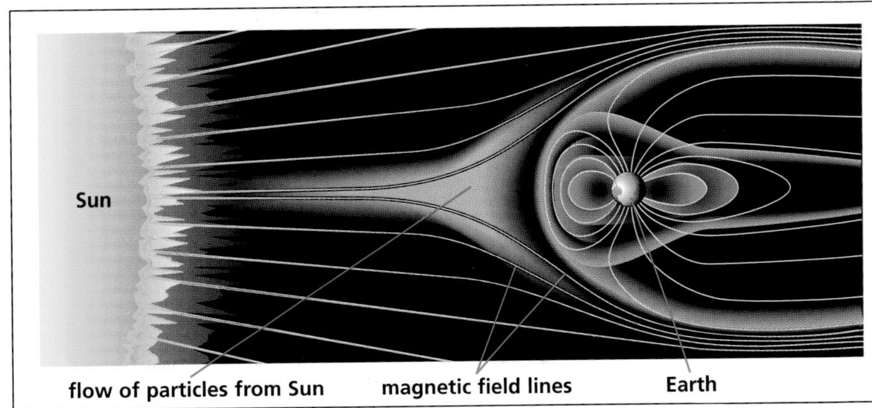

MAGNETIC EARTH

A large core of molten iron inside the Earth makes the whole planet strongly magnetic. Magnetic compasses point north because of this magnetism. It also influences the flow of gases from the Sun. Particles streaming from the Sun are deflected by the magnetism, like water round the bow of a ship. Auroras (northern or southern lights) are one of the results of the magnetism.

the Earth's atmosphere is 78 per cent nitrogen, 21 per cent oxygen, and 1 per cent water vapour, with tiny amounts of other gases. Humans and most other animals depend on oxygen to breathe.

Earth's only satellite, the Moon is at the same distance from the Sun as the Earth but it is too small to have enough gravity for an atmosphere. Without one, the Moon is dry, dead and inhospitable.

Born from dust

The Earth formed from the disc of dust and gas around the Sun about 4600 million years ago. When it first formed, the Earth was much hotter than it is now. The atmosphere was made up of nitrogen, water vapour and carbon dioxide belched out by volcanoes.

As the Earth started to cool, the water vapour formed the oceans. Life began in the oceans about 4 billion years ago. Over millions of years, early sea life and the first plants reduced the carbon dioxide in the air and produced great amounts of oxygen.

A changing planet

The Earth is still changing. Moving continents are building new mountains. Volcanoes erupt frequently. Weather and water wear away the surface and change the shape of the landscape.

The Earth had its share of craters when rocks were crashing on to both the Earth and the Moon thousands of millions of years ago. Little has changed on the Moon, but the Earth has altered so much that only faint outlines of about 100 craters can be identified today.

▲ The coloured glow of an aurora. These lights in the atmosphere are most often seen in the far north and far south. The photo shows a northern aurora.

THE RED PLANET

A bleak desert landscape stretches to the horizon on every side. The rust-coloured surface is littered with boulders but there is no sign of life. This place might be somewhere on Earth, but it is Mars.

Mars is the fourth planet out from the Sun. It is visible in our night sky, glowing orange-red, for a few weeks about every two years. Mars is the planet most like Earth. Its polar caps grow and shrink with the seasons. There is an atmosphere and weather. Mist forms in the morning and clouds sometimes shroud the tops of mountains. Strong winds whip up great dust storms.

But Mars is not a friendly place for life. The atmosphere is mainly carbon dioxide and very thin: the Earth's atmosphere is 100 times denser. Temperatures can reach 20°C on a summer afternoon, but are mostly much lower, less than –23°C on average.

In this environment, any liquid water would evaporate directly. However, there could be ice trapped in the rocks underground, and there is permanent water ice over the north pole. The frost that settles on the polar caps in winter is solid carbon dioxide, or 'dry ice'.

▲ This view of Mars was taken by the Hubble Space Telescope in 1995. On the far left (arrowed), the peak of a volcano pokes through early morning mist made of water ice crystals.

MARS DATA
Diameter at equator: 6796 km
Average distance from Sun: 228 million km
Time taken to spin on axis: 24.6 hours
Density (water = 1): 3.9
Time taken to orbit the Sun: 1.88 years
Moons: 2

▼ This panoramic view of a dried-up flood plain on Mars was taken by the space probe *Mars Pathfinder* in 1997. The red colour of the rocks is due to iron oxide: rust.

Martian history

Mars was a very different planet 1000 million years ago. At that time it had active volcanoes, a thicker atmosphere and flowing water. Long snaking valleys were cut by streams. Massive floods wore away parts of the ground and carried rocks about.

Several vast volcanoes rise over the plains in the northern hemisphere. None of them are active any longer. Olympus Mons is the largest volcanic mountain in the Solar System.

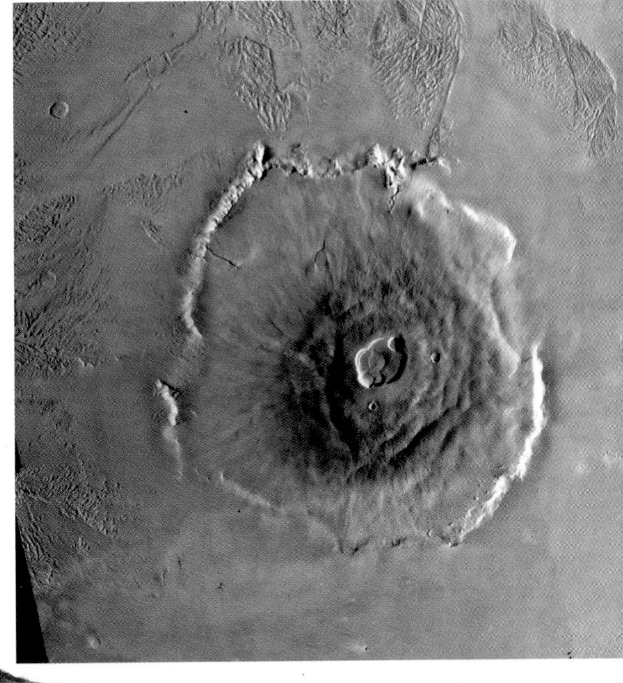

▶ Olympus Mons seen from orbit by *Viking* spacecraft. Mars has lower gravity than the Earth because it is a smaller planet. The low gravity helped Olympus Mons pile up to a stupendous height after many eruptions.

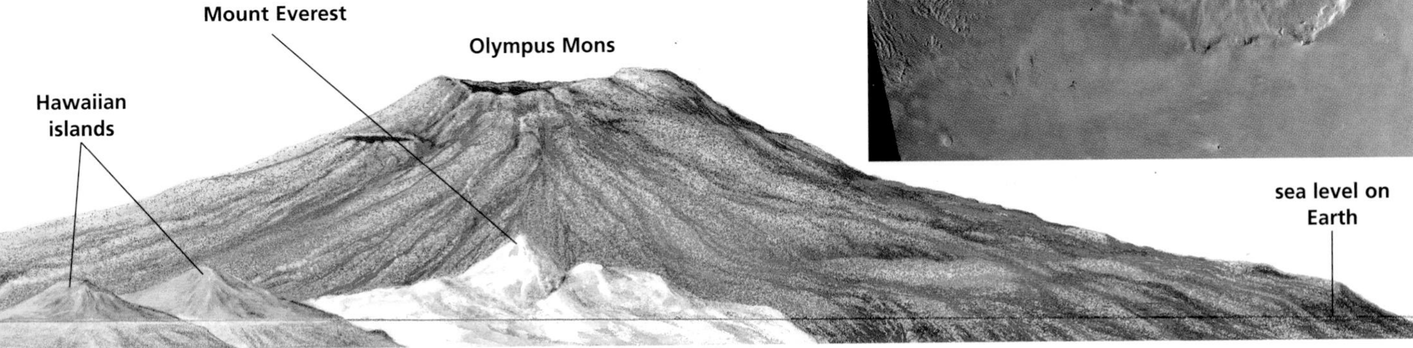

▲ The Martian volcano, Olympus Mons is 600 kilometres across and 25 kilometres high. The cliffs around its base are 6 kilometres high. Earth's largest volcano, Mauna Loa in Hawaii, rises just 10 kilometres above the surrounding seabed.

Canyons and craters

A huge system of canyons, called the Mariner Valleys, extends for 5000 kilometres near the equator. These great chasms are 6 kilometres deep on average. They formed when volcanic activity caused large areas of Mars's surface to bulge upwards. The Mariner Valleys are where the surface rocks cracked apart under the strain.

There are many craters on Mars. Most are in the southern hemisphere. In the north, craters have been covered up by flows of volcanic lava.

Is there life?

For a long time, people imagined there could be life on Mars. However, by the 1960s astronomers realized that there could be no liquid water there, which is needed by life as we know it.

If there ever was life on Mars, when it was warmer and wetter, there may be fossils waiting to be discovered. And it is just possible that some microscopic life could exist underground.

key words

- atmosphere
- carbon dioxide
- dust storms
- planet
- volcanoes

MARTIAN MOONS

Mars has two small moons, Phobos (right) and Deimos. Phobos is 28 kilometres long and Deimos 16 kilometres long. They could be asteroids captured by Mars's gravity. Both moons are very dark and covered in impact craters. Deimos looks smoother because it is covered by a layer of dust.

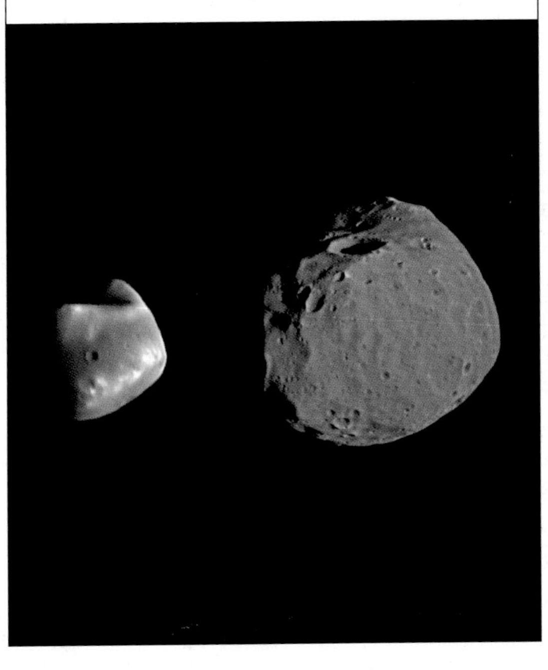

THE GIANT PLANET

Ferocious winds blowing at 400 kilometres per hour race around Jupiter's Great Red Spot. This is an immense storm that has been raging for more than 300 years on the Solar System's largest planet. Jupiter is 11 times larger than the Earth. Two planet Earths could fit side by side inside the Great Red Spot alone.

Jupiter is the fifth planet out from the Sun. Colourful bands of swirling clouds circle Jupiter. They are driven along by winds of up to 700 kilometres per hour, which are whipped up because the planet is spinning very quickly. The clouds are made of frozen crystals of water, ammonia and other chemicals, floating in an atmosphere of hydrogen and helium.

JUPITER DATA
Diameter at equator: 142,984 km
Average distance from Sun: 778.3 million km
Time taken to spin on axis: 9.9 hours
Density (water = 1): 1.3
Time taken to orbit the Sun: 11.86 years
Moons: 28

◀ An image of part of Jupiter, taken in 1994. Pieces of Comet Shoemaker-Levy 9 crashed down a few days before and the darker areas towards the bottom of the picture mark one of the impacts.

▼ There is no solid surface on Jupiter. Going down through the atmosphere, the gas gradually becomes thicker until it merges into the vast ball of liquid around Jupiter's small rocky core.

Inside Jupiter

Jupiter contains twice as much material as all the other planets put together. Most of it is hydrogen, though right at the centre of the planet there is a rocky core. Beneath the atmosphere, the hydrogen is squeezed by Jupiter's powerful gravity and made into a liquid.

Deep inside Jupiter, the liquid hydrogen is rather like a molten metal. It can conduct electricity and it makes Jupiter very magnetic. Jupiter's magnetism is 4000 times stronger than the Earth's. One effect of the magnetism is to turn Jupiter into a strong radio transmitter. Its signals can be picked up by radio telescopes.

◀ A view of Jupiter showing the Great Red Spot.

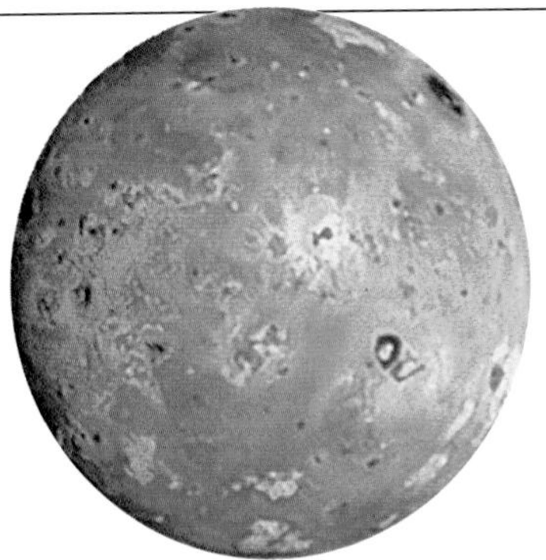

◀ Jupiter's volcanic moon, Io. The volcanoes produce the material sulphur. Sulphurous chemicals give Io its colourful appearance, shading it cream, yellow and orange.

▶ Europa's cracked and ridged surface shows signs of a liquid ocean of water underneath a thick crust of ice.

◀ Jupiter's moon Ganymede. Gigantic Ganymede has some cratered parts, but also has lighter coloured areas, where there are grooves rather than craters.

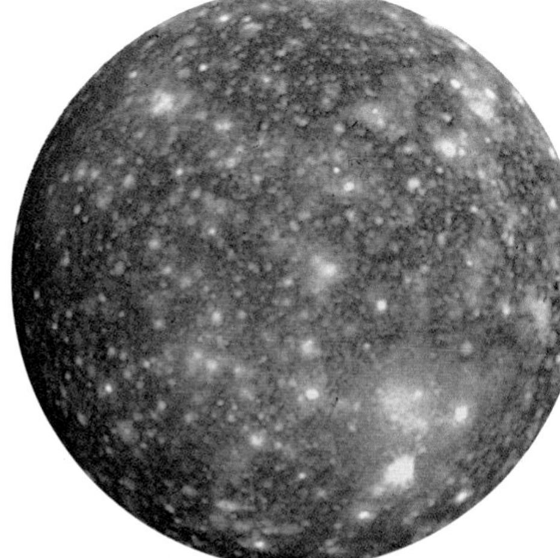

▶ Callisto is the most cratered world in the Solar System. Like Ganymede and Europa, it is made up of ice and rock.

key words

- atmosphere
- magnetism
- moons
- planet
- volcano

Jupiter's four largest moons – Io, Europa, Ganymede and Callisto – are known as the Galilean moons, because the astronomer Galileo Galilei was the first to observe them.

Space missions to Jupiter

The first spacecraft sent to explore Jupiter were *Pioneer* 10 and 11, launched in 1973 and 1974. They were followed by *Voyager* 1 and 2, which both flew past Jupiter in 1979 and sent back spectacular images. The *Voyager* pictures revealed that Jupiter, like all the giants, is surrounded by faint narrow rings made out of very fine dust. They also captured three small moons previously unknown to astronomers.

The *Galileo* spacecraft arrived at Jupiter in 1995. Instead of flying past like the earlier craft, it went into orbit so it could study the planet and its moons for several years. *Galileo* released a small probe that parachuted down into Jupiter's atmosphere. Its instruments collected information about the temperature, the pressure and the chemical composition, which was radioed back to Earth.

Jupiter's moons

Astronomers know of 28 moons orbiting Jupiter. Twenty-four of them are very small, with diameters ranging from 20 kilometres to 200 kilometres. The other four are far larger and can be seen through a small telescope. In order from Jupiter they are called Io, Europa, Ganymede and Callisto. Ganymede is the largest moon in the Solar System. At 5268 kilometres across, it is even larger than the planet Mercury.

Fire and ice

Io is an extraordinary world speckled with numerous active volcanoes that often spew out sulphurous chemicals. Nearby Europa is completely different. It has a thick crust of ice, but it is broken up in places and crossed by ridges, as if liquid water has oozed up from beneath and then frozen. It might even be a place where life could have started.

THE RINGED PLANET

Saturn's rings are spectacular. Though solid-looking, they are swarms of icy chunks orbiting Saturn like countless miniature moons. Saturn's beautiful rings make it easy to forget that the planet itself, second largest in the Solar System, is magnificent.

Like Jupiter, Saturn is a giant planet, made up mostly of liquid and gas. Its material is so light overall that Saturn would float in an ocean of water large enough to take it!

The clouds in Saturn's atmosphere lie under a layer of haze, which makes them look rather fuzzy. Saturn's rapid spin creates winds of up to 1600 kilometres per hour dragging the clouds into bands circling the planet. Saturn spins so fast that it bulges out around its equator. It is 11 per cent wider at its equator than between its poles.

key words

- moons
- planet
- rings

▼ This view of Saturn was taken by the Hubble Space Telescope in 1996. The large white spot close to the rings indicates a storm.

▼ Saturn's bright A and B rings are separated by a space called the Cassini Division. There are smaller gaps in the A and C rings. The rings are made up of pieces of ice, rock and dust.

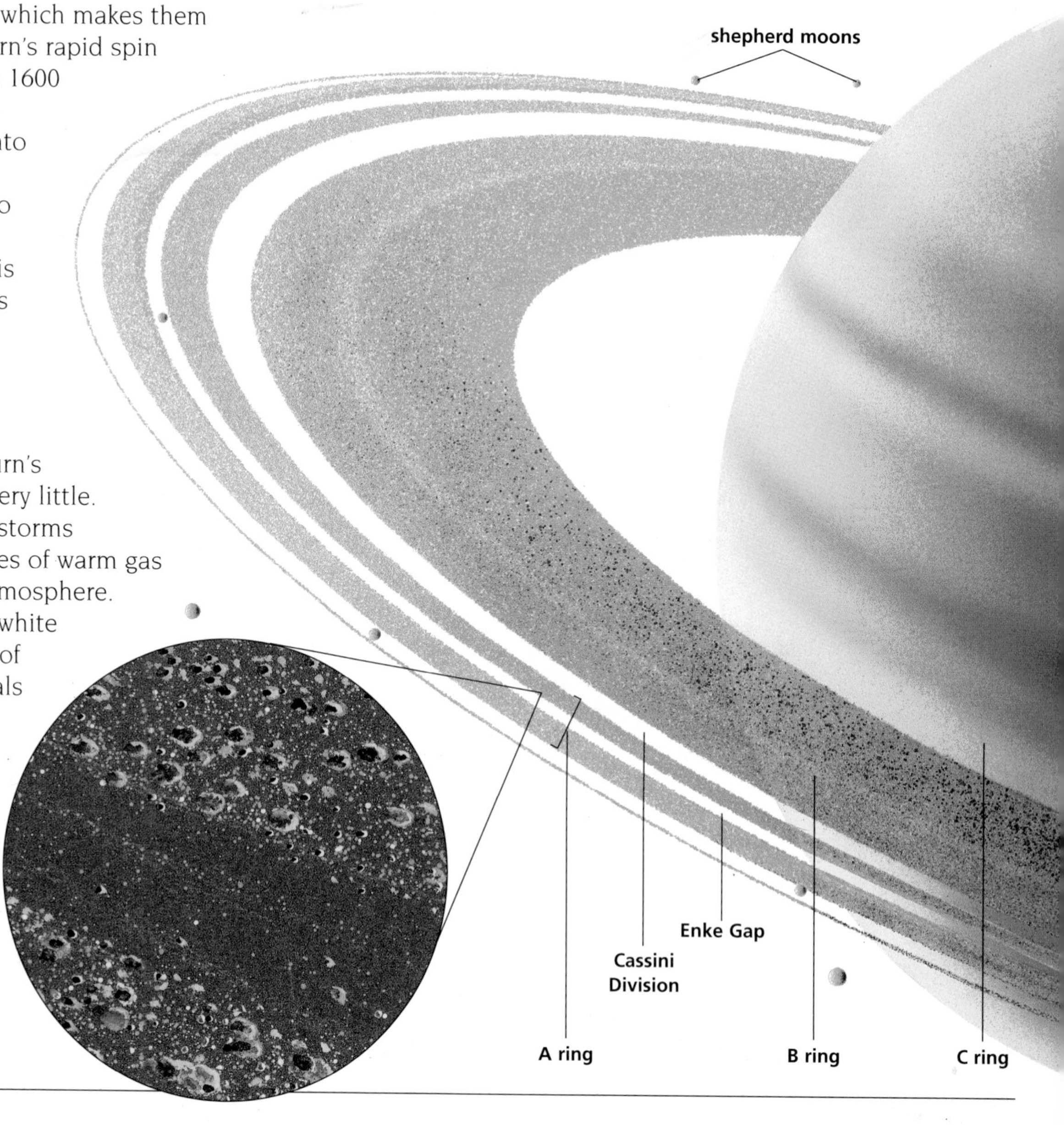

shepherd moons

Enke Gap

Cassini Division

A ring

B ring

C ring

Stormy weather

Most of the time, Saturn's appearance changes very little. About every 30 years, storms break out when bubbles of warm gas rise up through the atmosphere. We see them as large white spots because clouds of frozen ammonia crystals form over the storm areas. Since it takes Saturn about 30 years to orbit the Sun, the storms seem to be linked to Saturn's seasons.

▶ A close-up view of one of the rings.

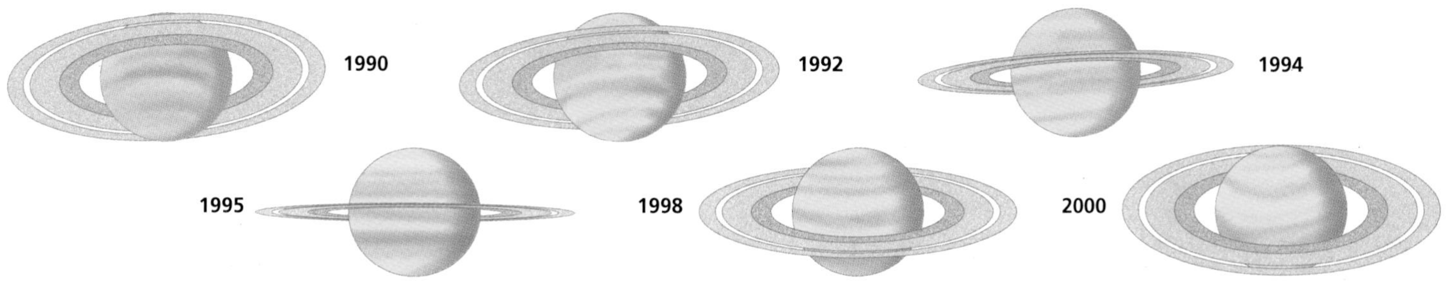

▲ Our angle of view of the rings changes as Saturn travels around the Sun. Most of the time they are easy to see with a small telescope. Every 15 years the rings seem to close up until they are edge-on to us. Since they are only a few metres thick, they become invisible for a while.

Rings

The icy lumps that make up Saturn's rings are frozen water with rock and dust mixed in. They range from pieces the size of a golf ball up to house-sized boulders. A few may be a kilometre across.

The three brightest rings are called A, B and C. Beyond them, dimmer and dustier rings extend outwards nearly 500,000 kilometres from Saturn's centre. Another dim ring, labelled D, lies closer to Saturn inside the C ring.

What look like gaps between the rings are not completely empty, but they contain far fewer objects. They are kept clear by the gravity of some of Saturn's moons. Two tiny moons, Pandora and Prometheus, keep the narrow F ring in place. For this reason they are called 'shepherd moons'.

Moons

The 13 moons nearest Saturn orbit within the ring system. Some of them actually share orbits, in twos and threes, though they avoid colliding with each other.

All the moons seen by the *Voyager* spacecraft are icy, with craters. Some also have smooth plains. The most mysterious is Titan. It is the second largest moon in the Solar System after Jupiter's moon Ganymede, but its surface is completely hidden by a blanket of smog. It is the only moon with a thick atmosphere.

Titan's atmosphere is half as thick again as the Earth's and, like the Earth's, is made mainly of nitrogen. But it also includes methane, the natural gas used for fuel on Earth. Astronomers suspect there could be lakes on Titan made of liquid methane and ethane. At the temperature of Titan (−180 °C) these chemicals will be liquid while water will be frozen rock hard.

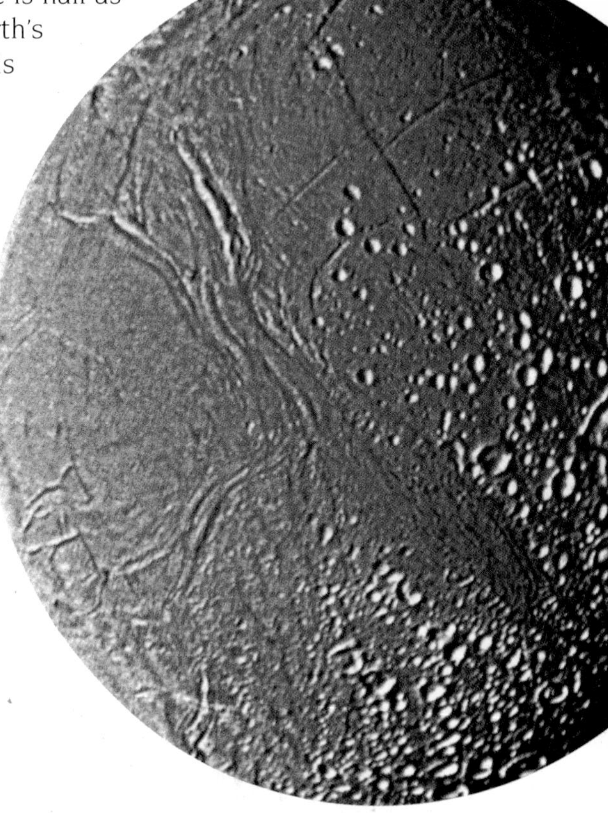

▼ The icy surface of Saturn's moon Enceladus is brighter than any other in the Solar System. It may be kept fresh by deposits of frost spewed out from ice volcanoes. Parts of the surface are cratered. There are also smooth plains where the craters have been covered.

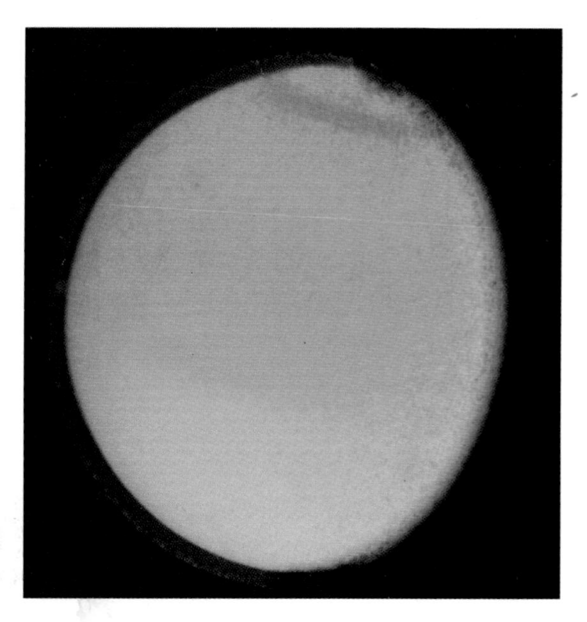

◀ Saturn's largest moon, Titan, has a thick atmosphere. The surface is hidden by orange haze.

SATURN DATA
Diameter at equator: 129,660 km
Average distance from Sun: 1427 million km
Time taken to spin on axis: 10.5 hours
Density (water = 1): 0.7
Time taken to orbit the Sun: 29.46 years
Moons: 30

A PLANET ON ITS SIDE

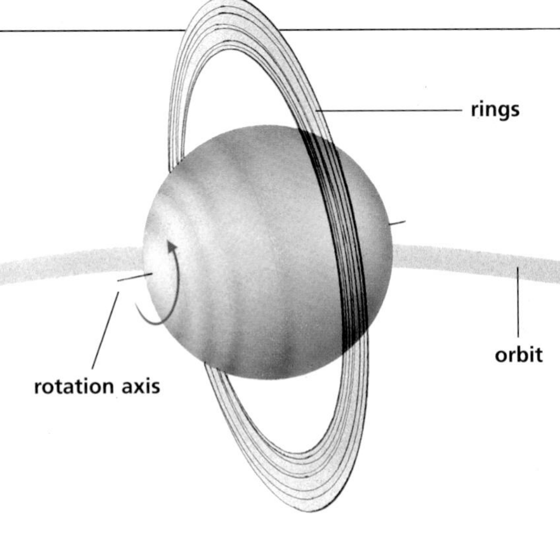

Tilted over on its side, Uranus has extraordinary seasons. Night and day each last 42 years at its north and south poles. The sixth planet from the Sun, Uranus is about four times larger than the Earth. The planet was discovered by the German-born astronomer William Herschel in 1781. It made him world famous.

To human eyes Uranus is a plain blue disc with no spots or bands. There is a rocky core at its centre. Over that lies a thick layer made chiefly of water. On the outside there is a thick atmosphere of hydrogen and helium.

key words
- infrared
- moon
- planet
- rings
- tilted axis

▲ With its spin axis tilted right over, Uranus seems to roll around its orbit lying on its side. It was probably knocked over in a great collision when the planets were first forming.

▶ William Herschel discovered Uranus using a homemade telescope. He also found the planet's two largest moons, Titania and Oberon.

Narrow rings

A set of narrow rings surrounds Uranus's equator. Of the nine main rings, one is 100 kilometres wide, and the others only 10 kilometres.

The rings are very dark. They are made of boulders about a metre across. In 1986, the *Voyager 2* spacecraft spotted more faint rings made of dust.

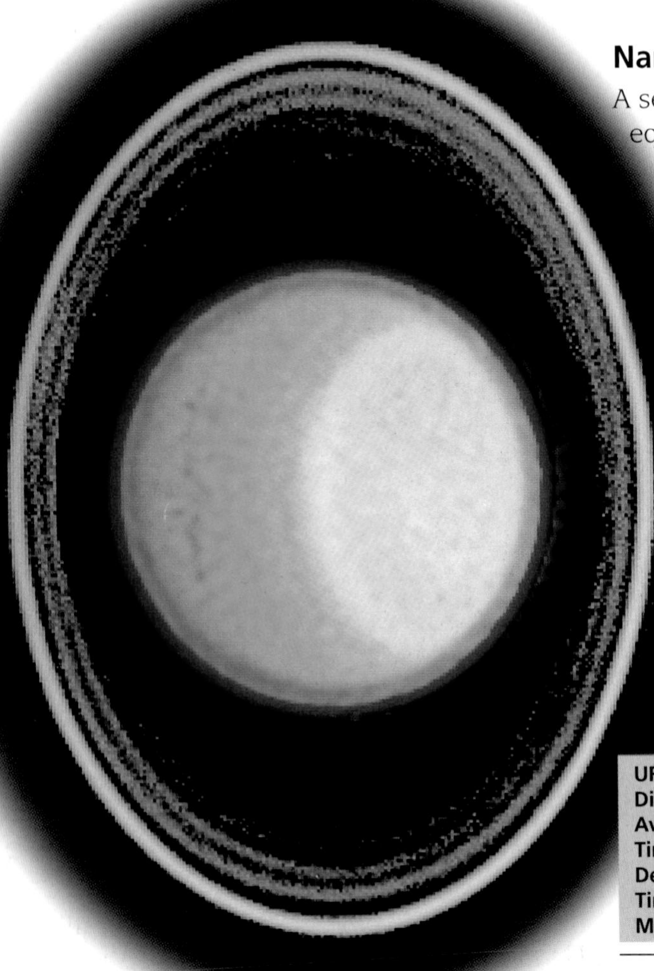

◀ A colour-coded infra-red picture of Uranus, showing the different layers of the atmosphere. Red is thin, high haze. Yellow is a cap of thicker haze over the planet's south pole. Blue is where the atmosphere is clearest.

URANUS DATA
Diameter at equator: 51,118 km
Average distance from Sun: 2871 million km
Time taken to spin on axis: 17.2 hours
Density (water = 1): 1.3
Time taken to orbit the Sun: 84.01 years
Moons: 21

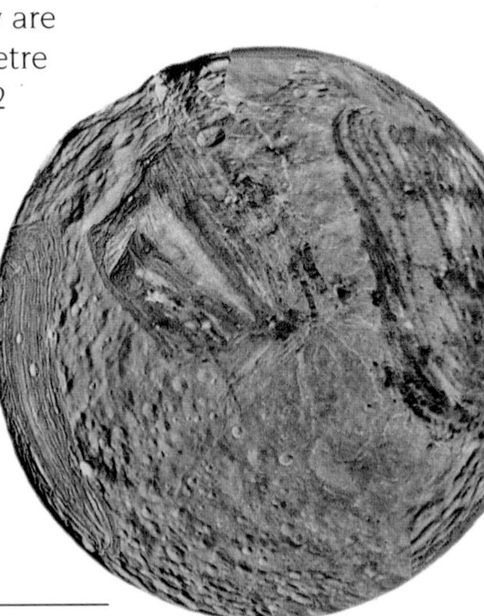

▲ Uranus's moon Miranda. Though only 472 kilometres across, its icy surface is an amazing jumble of different landscapes.

A WINDSWEPT PLANET

Windy weather is always the forecast for Neptune. Almost the whole planet is swept by jet streams blowing many times faster than any winds on Earth.

Eighth planet from the Sun, Neptune is about the same size as Uranus, and very similar inside. But much more goes on in Neptune's atmosphere than on Uranus. Stormy dark spots appear. Bands and patches of cloud are constantly changing. Both planets look blue because of methane gas in their atmospheres.

Neptune was discovered by Johann Galle in 1846 at the Berlin Observatory. Mathematicians were able to predict where it should be found because of the way its gravity affects Uranus's motion. The Voyager 2 spacecraft discovered that Neptune has several dark, narrow rings.

Triton

Seven small moons and one large one, Triton, orbit Neptune. Triton's diameter is 2705 kilometres, about four-fifths the size of the Earth's Moon. Though two-thirds of it are rock, its surface layer is icy. At a temperature of –236 °C, it is the coldest place ever recorded. It has a very thin atmosphere, which is mainly nitrogen.

When Triton's icy crust is warmed by the Sun, pockets of gas form in the frozen nitrogen. They erupt, sending geysers 8 kilometres high shooting upwards. Particles carried by the gas drift in the wind. Then they fall, leaving dark trails across the surface.

▲ Neptune's largest moon, Triton. This close-up image was taken by *Voyager 2*.

key words

- geysers
- methane
- storms

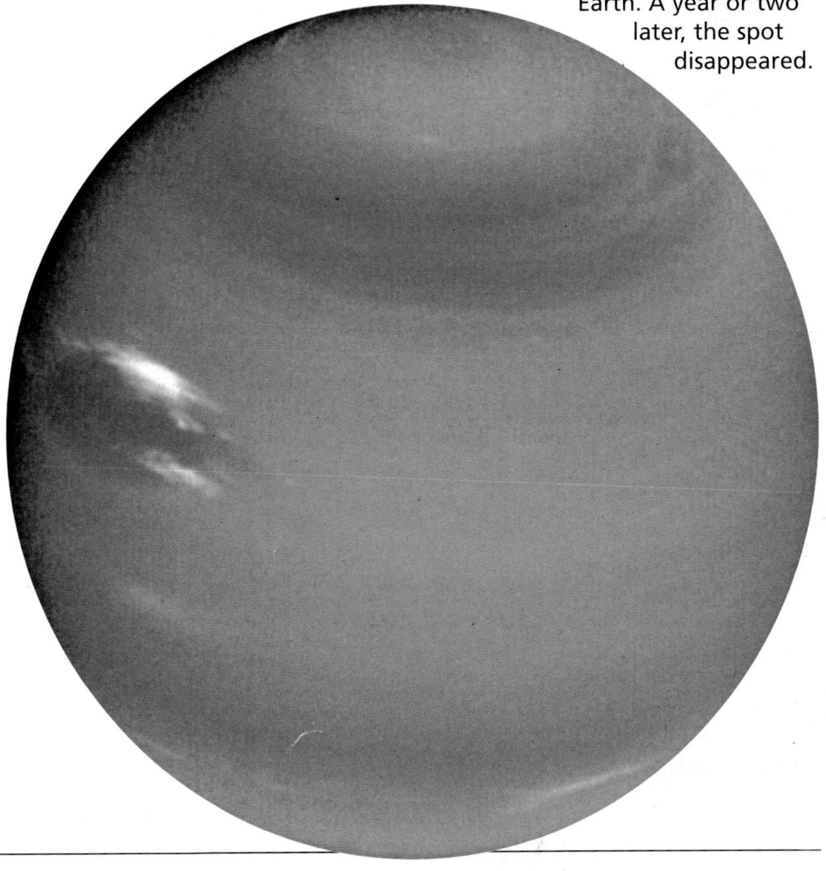

▼ Neptune as it looked when *Voyager 2* flew past it in 1989. The dark oval is where a storm formed. Called the Great Dark Spot, it was more than twice the size of the Earth. A year or two later, the spot disappeared.

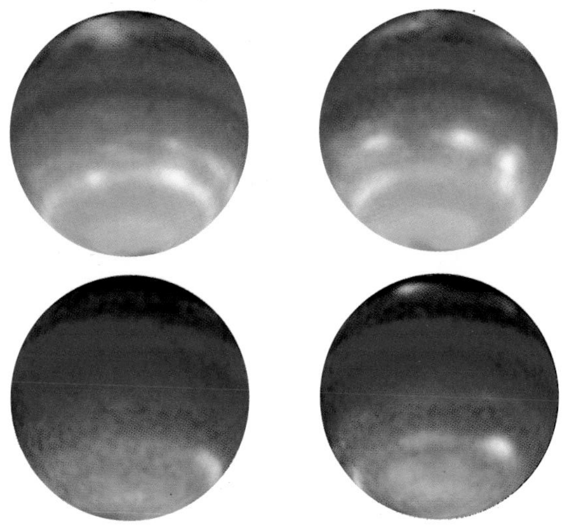

▲ Pictures from the Hubble Space Telescope show that dark spots and bright clouds come and go regularly in Neptune's atmosphere. The clouds are made of frozen crystals of methane.

NEPTUNE DATA
Diameter at equator: 49,532 km
Average distance from Sun: 4498 million km
Time taken to spin on axis: 16.1 hours
Density (water = 1): 1.64
Time taken to orbit the Sun: 165.8 years
Moons: 8

THE ICE DWARF

As soon as the American Clyde Tombaugh announced the discovery of the ninth planet in 1930, astronomers realized that Pluto was an oddity in the Solar System.

Pluto's orbit is different from those of the other planets. Its long, elliptical shape means that Pluto is sometimes nearer the Sun than Neptune. Its distance from the Sun varies between 7400 and 4400 million kilometres. Neptune and Pluto can never collide, though. In the time it takes Neptune to make three trips around the Sun, Pluto orbits exactly twice, so they never meet.

Pluto is by far the smallest planet but it is not rocky like the other small planets. Inside it is a mixture of ice and rock, with a thick layer of frozen water over the top. The world most similar to Pluto is Neptune's moon, Triton. Like Triton, Pluto has a very thin atmosphere of nitrogen.

Charon

Pluto's moon Charon was discovered in 1978. Then in 1992, astronomers started to find many miniature ice planets orbiting beyond Neptune. Charon could have become Pluto's moon when two of these small objects collided billions of years ago. A great crash could also explain why Pluto's axis is tilted by 58 degrees.

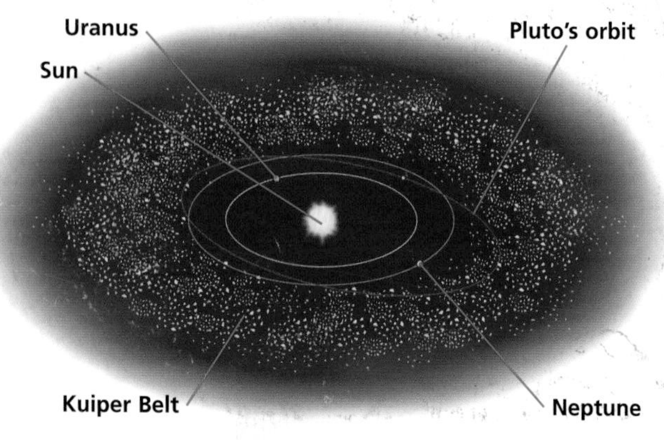

◀ Pluto is the largest known member of a family of thousands of icy miniature planets, which orbit the Sun in a belt beyond Neptune. This belt is called the Kuiper Belt.

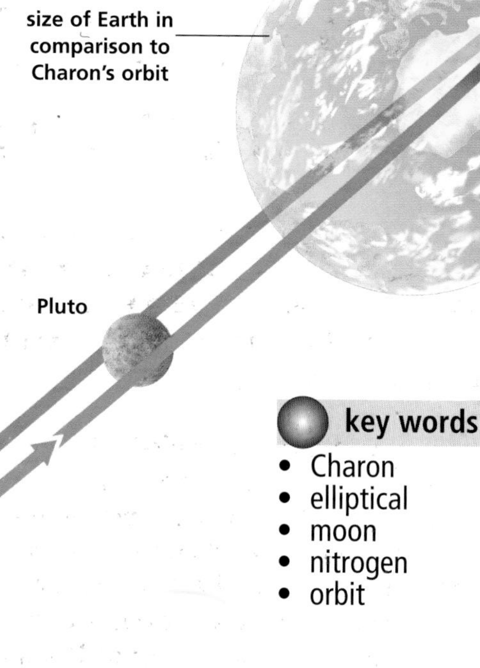

▶ Pluto is a tiny planet, smaller across than the United States. Pluto's moon Charon is half as big. The distance between them is only one and a half times the Earth's diameter. Charon orbits Pluto in 6.4 days. The same side of Charon always faces Pluto.

key words

- Charon
- elliptical
- moon
- nitrogen
- orbit

▼ The small photo is the most detailed picture ever taken of Pluto and Charon. It was made by the Hubble Space Telescope and shows just vague dark and light patches. The big picture shows what we think they may look like from other evidence. No spacecraft has yet visited Pluto.

PLUTO DATA
Diameter at equator: 2360 km
Average distance from Sun: 5900 million km
Time taken to spin on axis: 6.39 days
Density (water = 1): 1.83
Time taken to orbit the Sun: 247.7 years
Moons: 1

MINIATURE WORLDS

Millions of asteroids orbit the Sun in the asteroid belt between Mars and Jupiter. Though there are so many, all these small rocky chunks together would only make one seventh of our Moon.

The asteroids (sometimes called minor planets) are made of rock, metal or a mixture of both. They are small pieces left over from when the planets were forming 4600 million years ago. The first asteroid to be discovered was Ceres. It was found by the Italian astronomer Guiseppe Piazzi in 1801, while he was searching for planets between Jupiter and Mars. At 975 kilometres across, Ceres is the largest asteroid. The smallest ones are no bigger than boulders.

The largest asteroids are ball-shaped. Most have odd, elongated shapes. Spacecraft have returned detailed pictures of several asteroids. All of them are pitted with craters where smaller rocks have crashed into them.

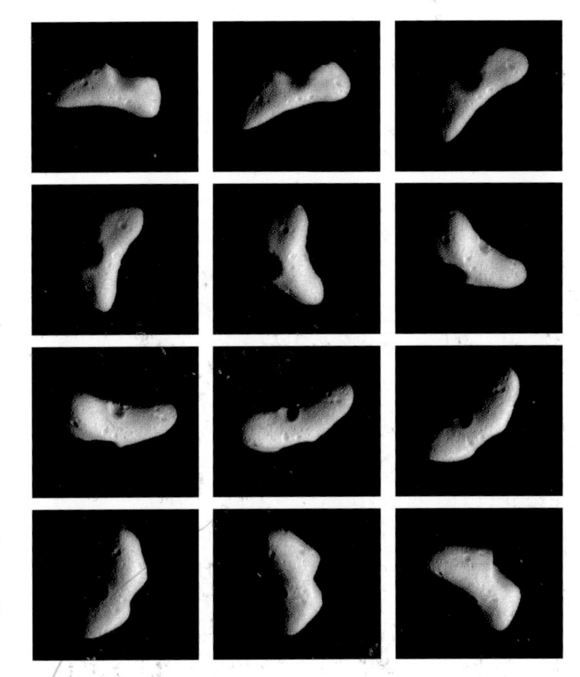

▶ Twelve views of the asteroid Eros. In February 2000 a spacecraft called *NEAR Shoemaker* went into orbit around Eros. Eros is 33 kilometres long and 13 kilometres wide.

key words

- asteroids
- craters
- minor planets

Unusual orbits

A few asteroids are in orbits outside the main asteroid belt. In 1994, a 10-metre-wide rock passed the Earth only 105,000 kilometres away – less than one third the distance to the Moon. Chiron is one of several distant asteroids with orbits between Jupiter and Uranus. Two clusters of asteroids, called the Trojans, orbit the Sun at exactly the same distance as Jupiter.

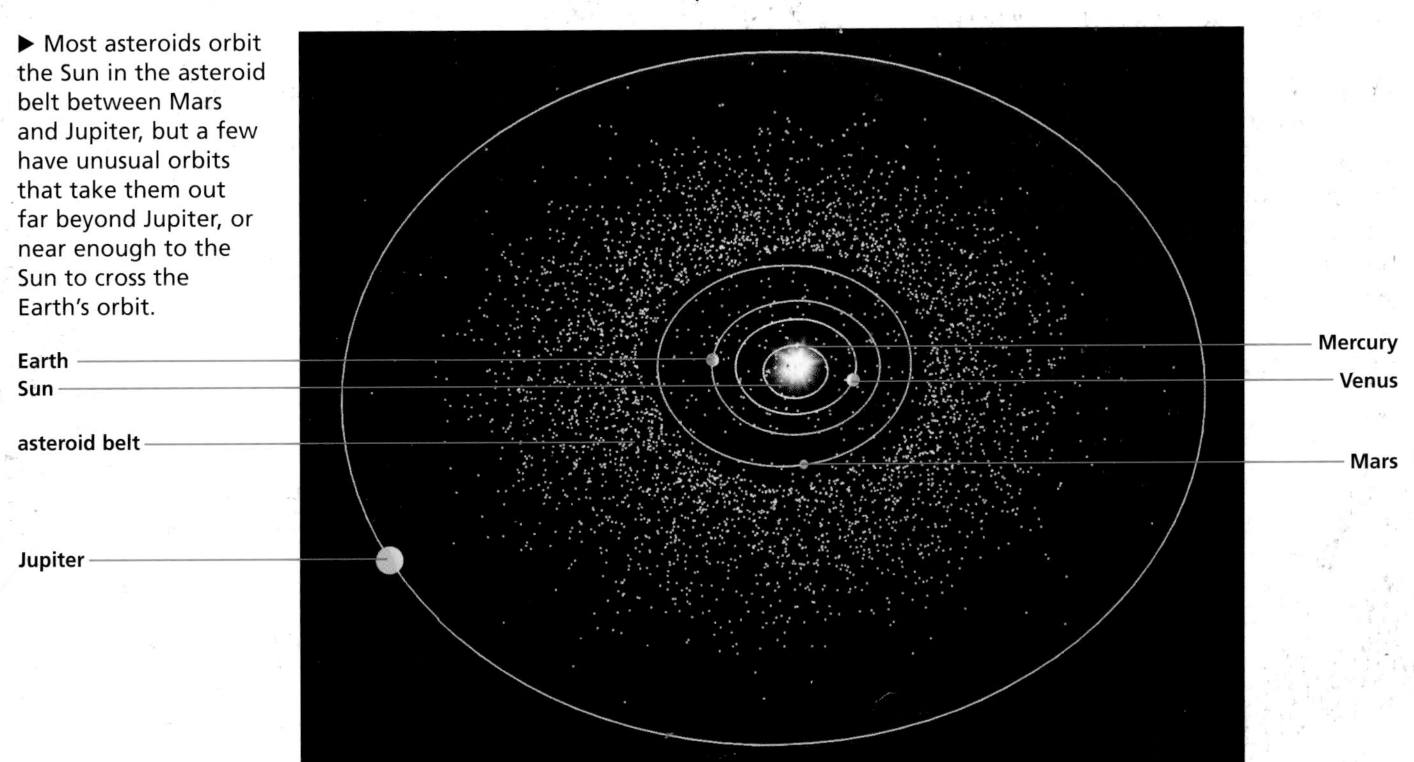

▶ Most asteroids orbit the Sun in the asteroid belt between Mars and Jupiter, but a few have unusual orbits that take them out far beyond Jupiter, or near enough to the Sun to cross the Earth's orbit.

TAILS ACROSS THE SKY

Not many sights in the night sky are as awesome as a bright comet. Often arriving without warning, a comet can inspire fear and wonder.

Though comets look spectacular, they contain very little material. The Earth has passed through the tail of a comet without any noticeable effect. Only the comet's nucleus is solid, made of a mixture of ice and dust. Photos of the nucleus of Halley's Comet taken by the spacecraft *Giotto* showed that it is only about 10 kilometres long.

Thousands of millions of comet nuclei swarm around the Solar System far beyond Neptune and Pluto. A few find their way to the inner Solar System. They generally sweep around the Sun then travel back out into space, not to return for thousands of years. But some are pulled off course by massive Jupiter's strong gravity. This changes their orbits. They stay nearer the Sun and are seen regularly every few years.

key words

- gravity
- nucleus
- orbit

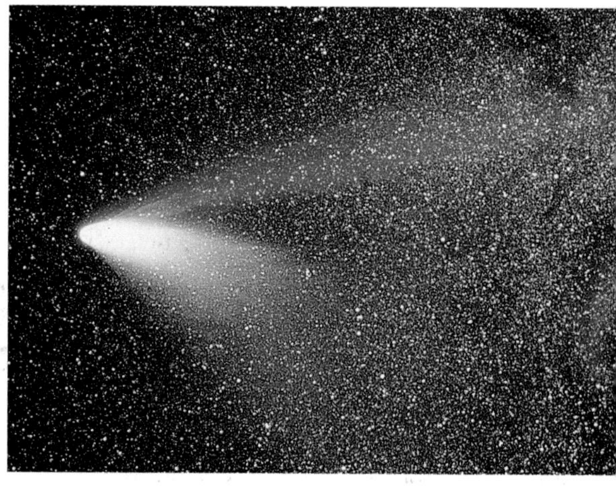

▲ Comet Hale-Bopp was an unusually bright comet seen by many people in 1997. Its dust tail is bright and curved. The fainter blue tail is gas. Radiation from the Sun makes it glow.

Parts of a comet

When a comet is warmed by the Sun, a large cloud of gas and dust, called the coma, comes off the central nucleus. The coma can be a million kilometres across. Sunlight and gas streaming from the Sun push the dust and gas away from the comet in two separate tails. The tails can grow to be hundreds of millions of kilometres long. The dust tail shines with reflected sunlight.

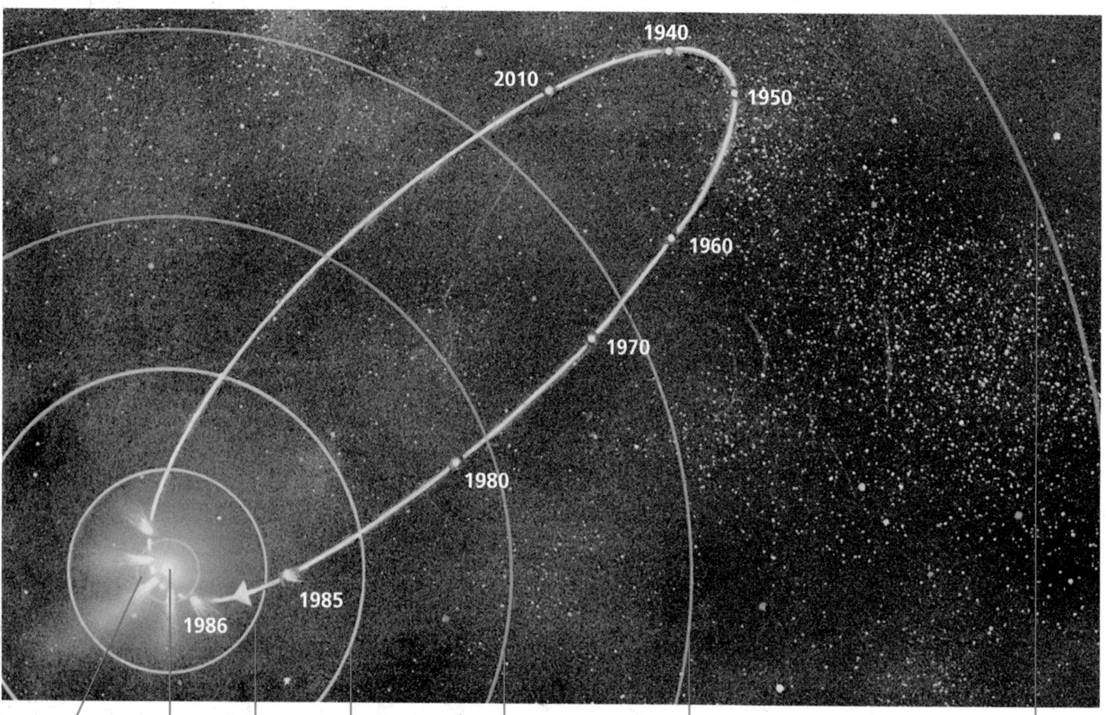

▼ Halley's Comet follows a long elliptical orbit around the Sun. It takes about 76 years to complete one orbit. The last time it came near the Sun and the Earth was in 1986. Several spacecraft were sent to study it.

▼ Edmond Halley (1656–1742) was the first person to calculate the path of a comet and predict when it would be seen again. Halley's Comet was named in his honour even though he did not discover it. Historical records show that Halley's Comet has been observed for more than 2000 years.

Space rocks

The Earth is constantly pelted by dust and bits of rock from space. On any dark night you could see a brilliant streak of light flash across the sky for a second or two, as a grain of dust burns up.

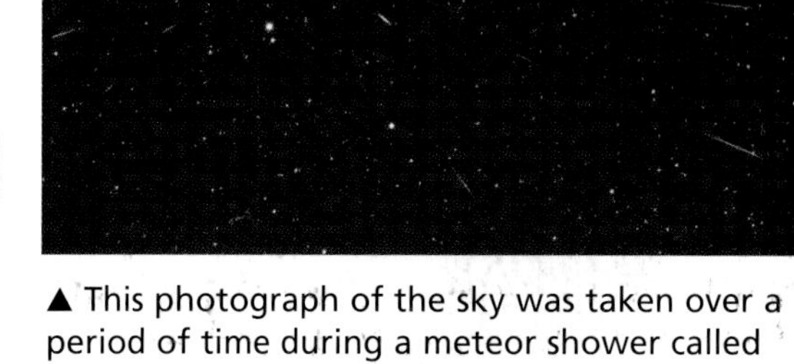

▲ This photograph of the sky was taken over a period of time during a meteor shower called the Leonids. The streaks that radiate outwards are meteor trails.

Streams of dust from comets circle around the Sun. Every year, the Earth ploughs through some of these streams on about the same dates, and we get showers of meteors (often called 'shooting stars'). The Eta Aquarid shower in May, for example, is caused by dust from Halley's Comet. Not all meteors come in showers, though. One-off meteors might be seen anywhere on any night.

Large dust grains burn up as they speed through the atmosphere about 100 kilometres up. But every year, millions of tonnes of very fine space dust drifts down on to the Earth without burning up.

key words

- craters
- meteorites
- meteors
- shooting stars

Meteorites

Sometimes, quite large rocks from space reach the ground. They are called meteorites. Some are stone, some metal, and some a mix of both. Not many are seen to fall, but there are certain places in the world where meteorites have lain undisturbed over many years and can be collected. Many have been recovered from the ice of Antarctica.

Careful study shows most meteorites have come from the asteroid belt, but a very few are definitely rocks that were once part of the Moon or Mars.

IMPORTANT METEOR SHOWERS

Name	Date seen
Quadrantids	4 January
Eta Aquarids	4 May
Perseids	12 August
Geminids	13 December

▼ A fragment of an iron meteorite. Some meteorites are made up of a particular mixture of iron and nickel, which produces the criss-cross pattern as seen here.

▼ Meteor Crater in Arizona, USA, was created when a 40-metre-wide iron meteorite crashed to Earth about 50,000 years ago. The crater is 1.2 kilometres across and 200 metres deep.

LIGHTS IN THE SKY

From red giants to white dwarfs, stars come in a variety of colours and a huge range of sizes. Like our Sun, every star is a giant ball of hot, glowing gas. But because they are so far away, we see them only as pinpricks of light.

Every star keeps shining for millions or billions of years because nuclear energy is generated inside it. But not all stars are identical. They come in different sizes and colours depending on how much material they contain. They also change size and colour as they get older.

The colour of a star tells us its surface temperature. The hottest stars are white or bluish and give off the most intense light, including strong, ultraviolet radiation. The coolest stars look red and their surfaces shine dimly. Many give out more infrared than visible light. Our yellow Sun is a middle-sized star.

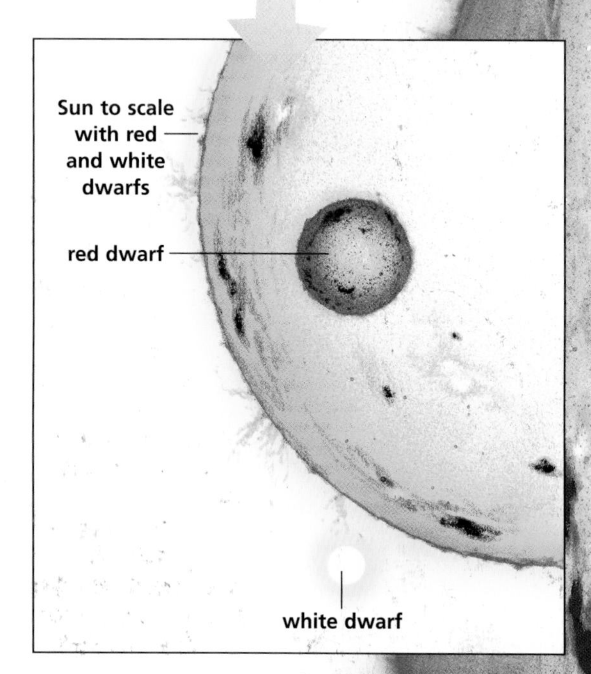

X-RAY BINARIES

In some binary stars, one of the pair is normal but the other is a collapsed star. The collapsed star has shrunk to become an immensely dense ball less than 10 kilometres across.

In such a binary pair, the very strong gravity of the collapsed star pulls hot gas away from the normal star as they circle each other. This material collects around the collapsed star, forming a flat disk. At the centre of the disk, extremely hot material falls on to the collapsed star, and energy is given out in the form of intense X-rays.

One kind of X-ray binary consists of a neutron star and a blue giant star (see below).

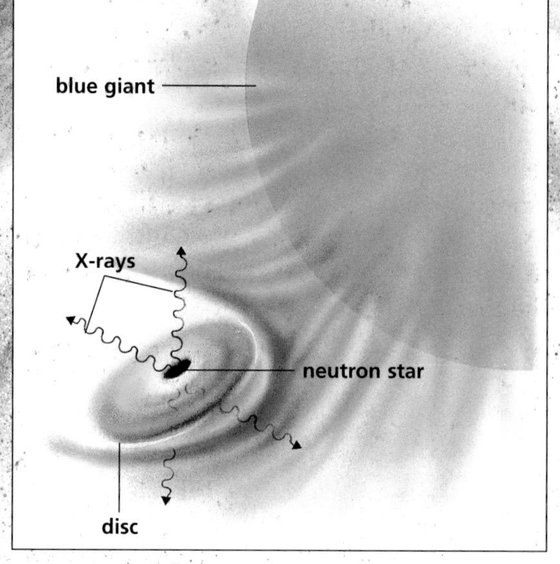

◀ Stars of different kinds, shown to scale. Our yellow-white Sun is a medium-sized star. The blue supergiant was born a giant, but the red supergiant used to be smaller and has swelled up. A red dwarf is an ordinary star, but a white dwarf is the core of a star that was once a red giant.

Double and variable stars

About half of all 'stars' in the sky are really a pair of stars, orbiting around the balancing point between them. They are often called binary stars. If their orbits are edge on towards us, the stars will alternately cross behind and in front of each other. When that happens, the total light from the two stars dips at regular intervals. Star couples like these are called eclipsing binaries.

The brightness of single stars can also change. Such stars are called variable stars. They change for many different reasons. Some giant stars gently pulse in and out every few days in a regular way. Most supergiants also pulsate slowly over several years, though in a pattern that is only partly regular.

Other stars suddenly brighten up or dim in an unpredictable way. One kind of supergiant forms tiny sooty particles in its outer layers. They make the star look much dimmer for a while until they are blown off into space.

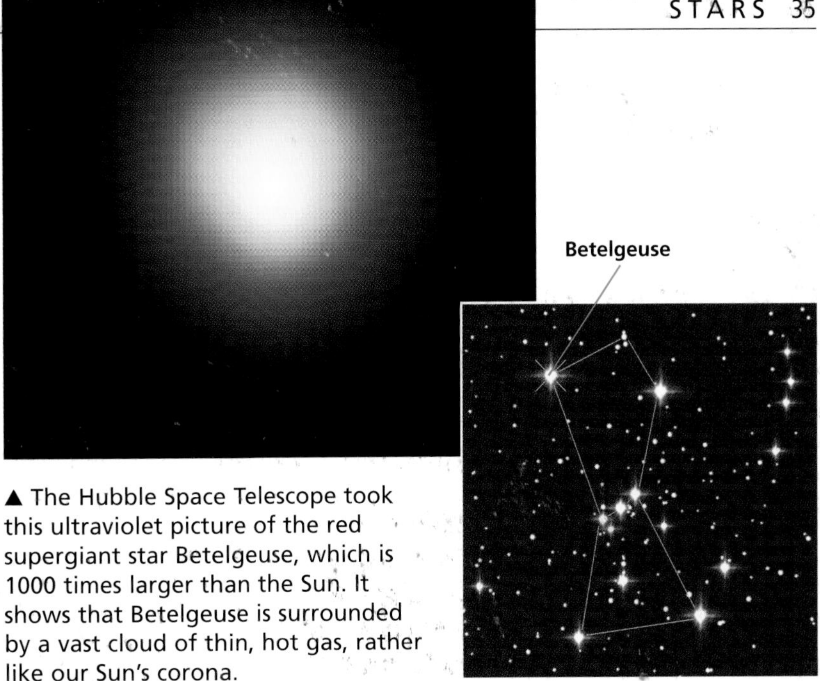

▲ The Hubble Space Telescope took this ultraviolet picture of the red supergiant star Betelgeuse, which is 1000 times larger than the Sun. It shows that Betelgeuse is surrounded by a vast cloud of thin, hot gas, rather like our Sun's corona.

SOME SPECIAL STARS

Name	What's special	Constellation
Sirius	brightest star	Canis Major
Canopus	second-brightest star	Carina
Alpha Centauri	third-brightest star	Centaurus
Proxima	nearest star (4 light years)	Centaurus
Algol	most famous eclipsing binary	Perseus
Mira	famous variable, the first discovered	Cetus

key words

- binary stars
- neutron stars
- red giants
- supergiants
- white dwarfs
- X-rays

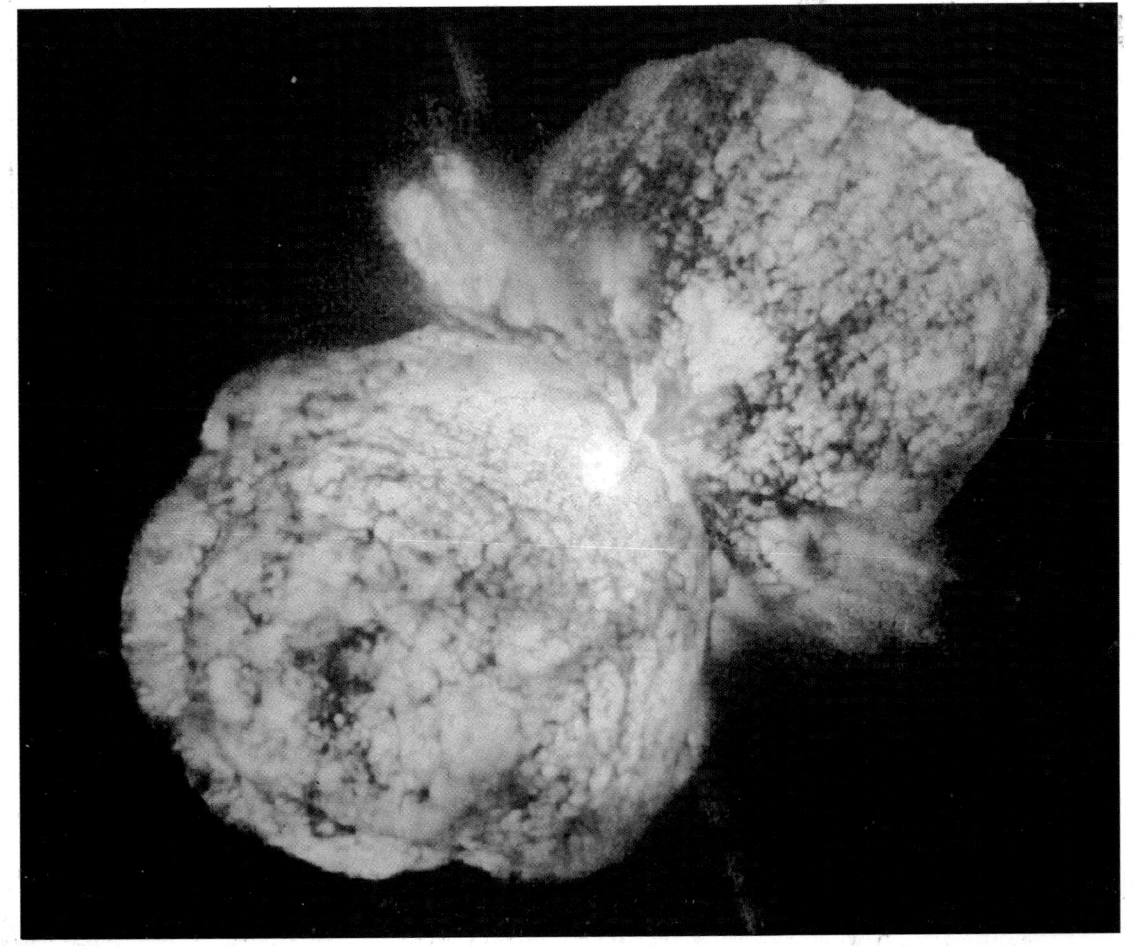

◀ These twin lobes of gas and dust, pictured by the Hubble Space Telescope, are flowing out from one of the most massive known stars, which is hidden inside. Called Eta Carinae, astronomers suspect it may be a double star. It radiates five million times more power than the Sun.

THE LIVES OF STARS

In the far future, the Sun's colour will gradually darken to orange and then red. It will swell until its outer layers reach as far as the Earth's orbit

Stars do not last forever. They are born and they die. Our Sun is about 5000 million years old now. It has another 5000 million to go before it swells into a red giant and its life as the yellow star we know comes to an end.

key words

- gravity
- mass
- neutron
- nuclear energy

A star's life

New stars are constantly being born to replace ones that die. Clusters of stars usually form together. They begin life in vast clouds of cold, dark gas and dust in space. Gravity pulls the material together into large, rotating clumps. As long as a gas clump is at least a twentieth the size of the Sun, it heats up enough inside to generate nuclear energy and become a star.

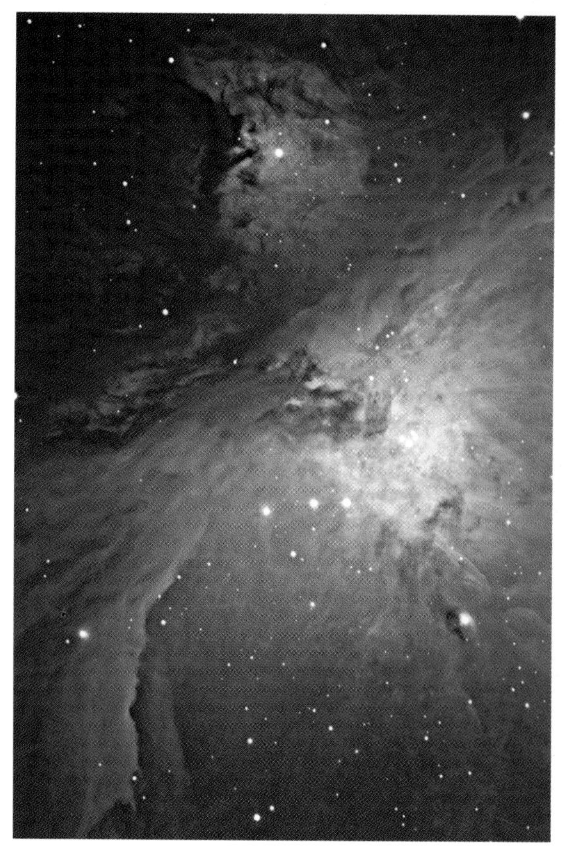

▶ The Orion Nebula is a huge, glowing bubble of gas lit up by a group of hot stars that were born only 100,000 years ago. More new stars are being created nearby. Some of them are surrounded by discs of gas and dust, where planets might form.

▼ Different kinds of star have different life cycles. The lives of a small and a large star are shown here.

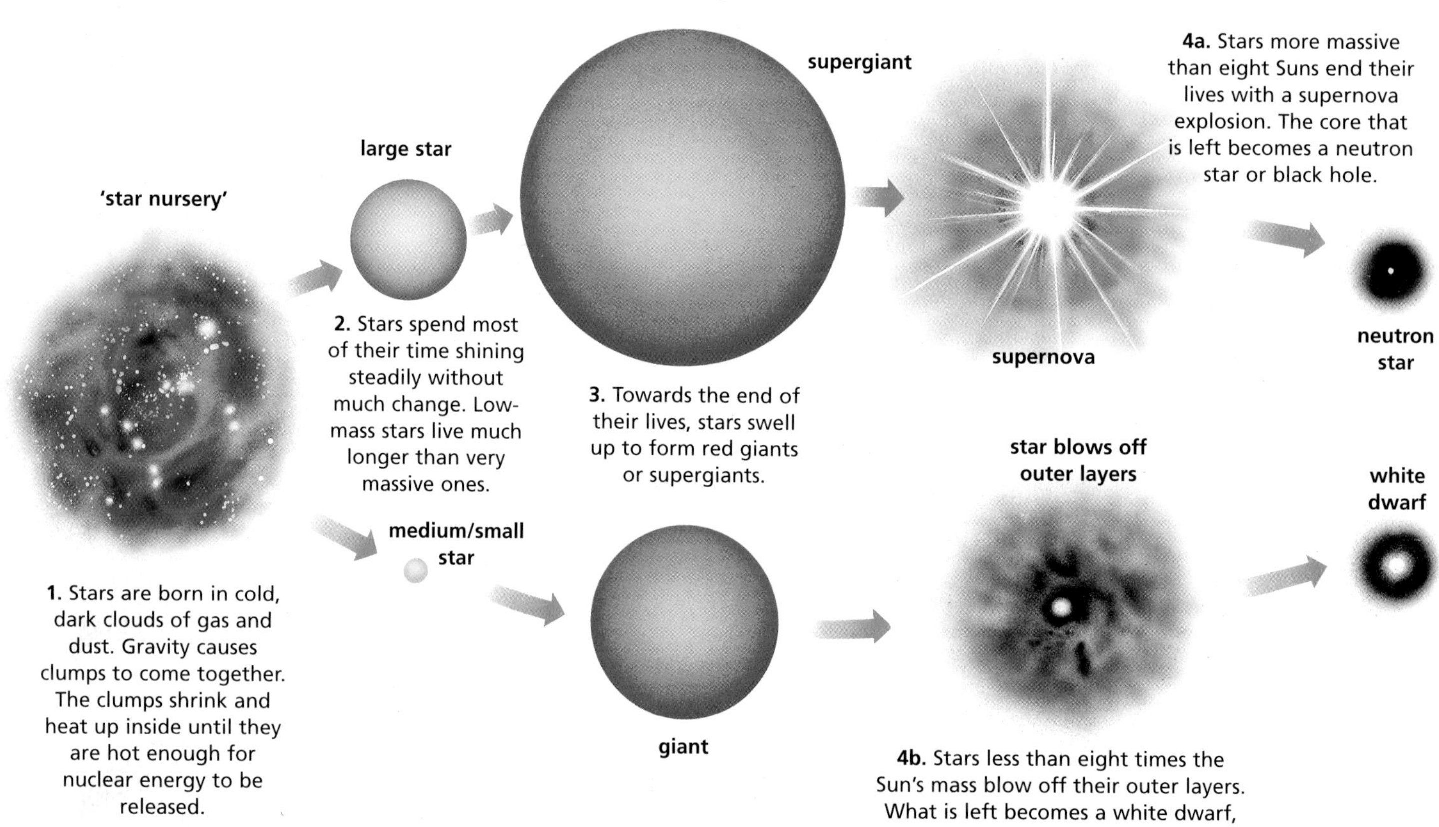

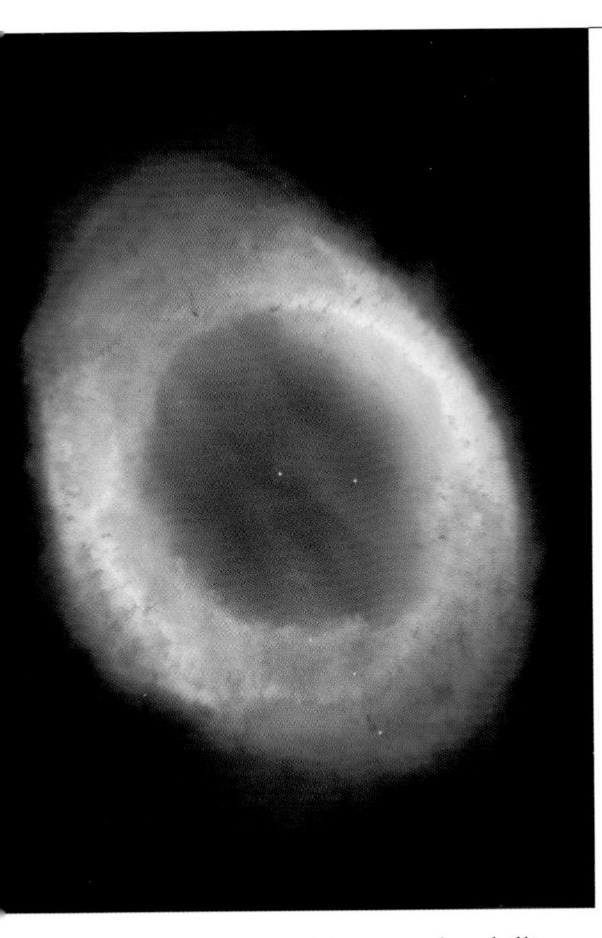

For most of their lifetime (often billions of years) stars shine steadily without much change. Smaller stars live much longer than very large ones. But when a star's nuclear fuel begins to run out, the star reacts by puffing up until it becomes a giant or a supergiant. Stars that are less than one and a half times the Sun's mass then blow off their outer layers, leaving a tiny, cooling star called a white dwarf. Stars that are more massive than one and a half Suns end their lives with a supernova explosion. The leftover core becomes a neutron star, or sometimes a black hole.

White dwarfs and neutron stars

The remains left behind when stars die are very strange objects. They collapse in on themselves and become incredibly dense. A white dwarf star, though similar in size to the Earth, has as much mass as the Sun. A teaspoonful would weigh many tonnes.

Neutron stars are even denser than white dwarfs. A neutron star is more massive (weighs more) than the Sun, but all this mass is packed into a ball just 10 kilometres or so across.

Black holes

If a very large star (more than eight times the Sun's mass) becomes a supernova, its core collapses totally. If the core is massive enough, it can form a black hole. A black hole is even more dense than a neutron star. The gravity around it is so immensely strong that not even light can escape. This makes it impossible to see. Black holes are only detected when they are paired with another star. Then, the effects they have can be seen.

◀ The Ring Nebula. The small dot in the centre is the remains of an old star that blew off its outside layers of gas between 5000 and 6000 years ago. It is now a white dwarf. Its ultraviolet radiation makes the nebula glow.

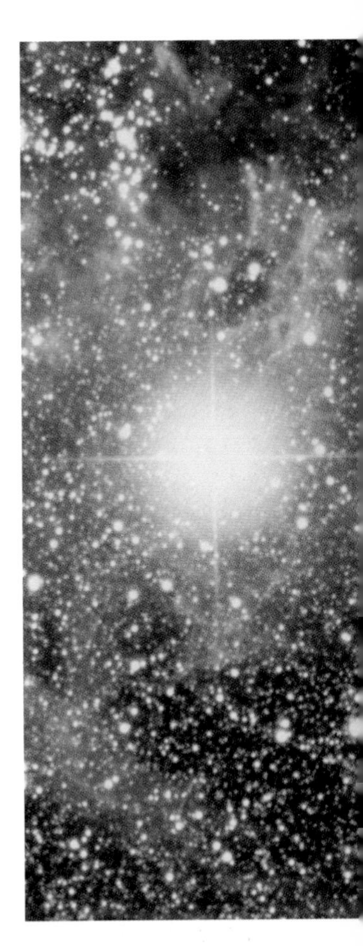

▶ A star in the small neighbouring galaxy called the Large Magellanic Cloud exploded in 1987. It was the brightest, nearest supernova observed since the year 1604.

▼ The Crab Nebula. This tangle of gas was created when a star exploded as a supernova in 1054. What was left of the star's core became a spinning neutron star.

GAS CLOUDS AND STAR CROWDS

Little swarms of glittering stars and shining clouds coloured pink and blue are dotted all through the Milky Way. These clusters and nebulas are some of the most beautiful sights in the sky.

The space between the stars is not completely empty. There are scatterings of gas molecules and tiny grains of dust. In some places the gas and dust have collected into immense, dark clouds.

Clouds between the stars and around individual stars are called nebulas. If there is a bright star nearby, a nebula shines. Ultraviolet starlight makes gas glow with its own light. Dust clouds shine because they reflect starlight.

Though dark nebulas do not give out any light, they may stand out as silhouettes against stars and glowing gas farther away. Unlike light, infrared radiation and radio waves can travel from inside dark nebulas to be picked up by telescopes on Earth.

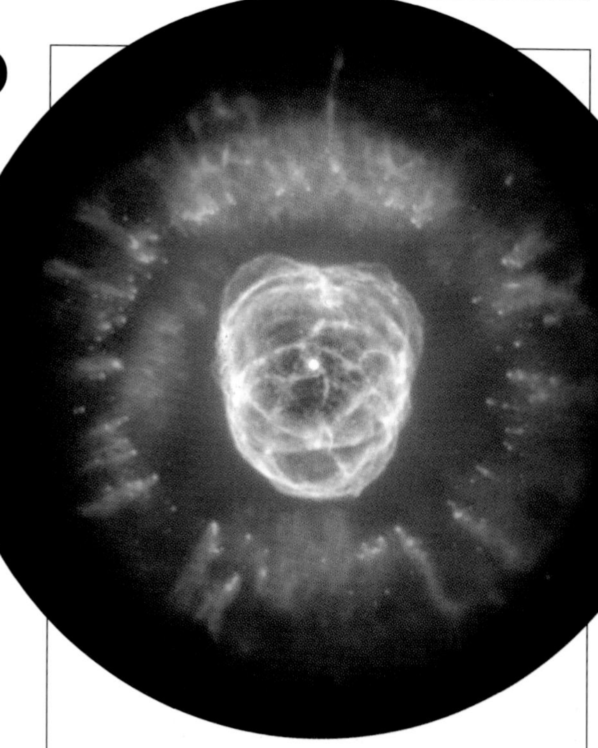

▶ The Eskimo Nebula, an example of a planetary nebula.

There is enough gas between the stars in the Milky Way to make 10 million Sun-sized stars.

PLANETARY NEBULAS

When a small or medium-sized star reaches the end of its life, it expands and the outer layers of gas are blown off into space. Nebulas of this kind are called 'planetary nebulas'. The name has nothing to do with planets: it was invented by the astronomer Sir William Herschel, because this type of nebula reminded him of planets.

◀ The Horsehead Nebula. The shape like a horse's head is a column of gas and dust projecting out of a large dark nebula, into the bright glowing nebula next to it.

Nebula nurseries

New stars are born inside dark nebulas. The powerful radiation given off by massive new stars opens up bubbles in the nebula and makes the gas glow. Most of the gas is hydrogen, which glows pink.

Bright nebulas are always near to young stars. A newly-formed star cluster can often be seen at the centre of a bright nebula. They are called open clusters. They contain between several hundred and several thousand stars.

key words

- infrared
- molecule
- radiation
- ultraviolet

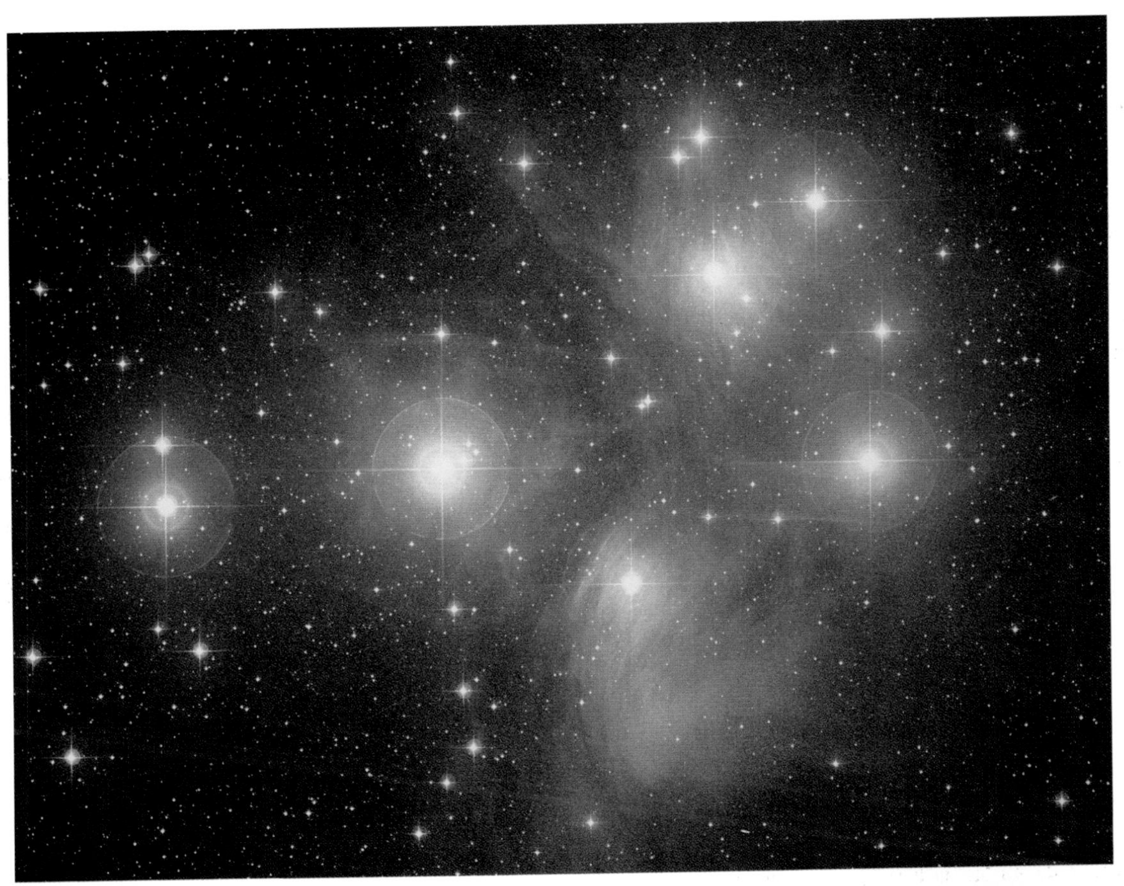

◀ The Pleiades. About 500 stars belong to this open star cluster, but only the brightest can be seen in this picture. The cluster is travelling through an interstellar cloud of gas and dust. The dust reflects the starlight to make a blue reflection nebula.

▼ The centre of a globular cluster of stars. This particular cluster is nicknamed the starfish, because of the bright stellar 'arms' that curve away from the centre.

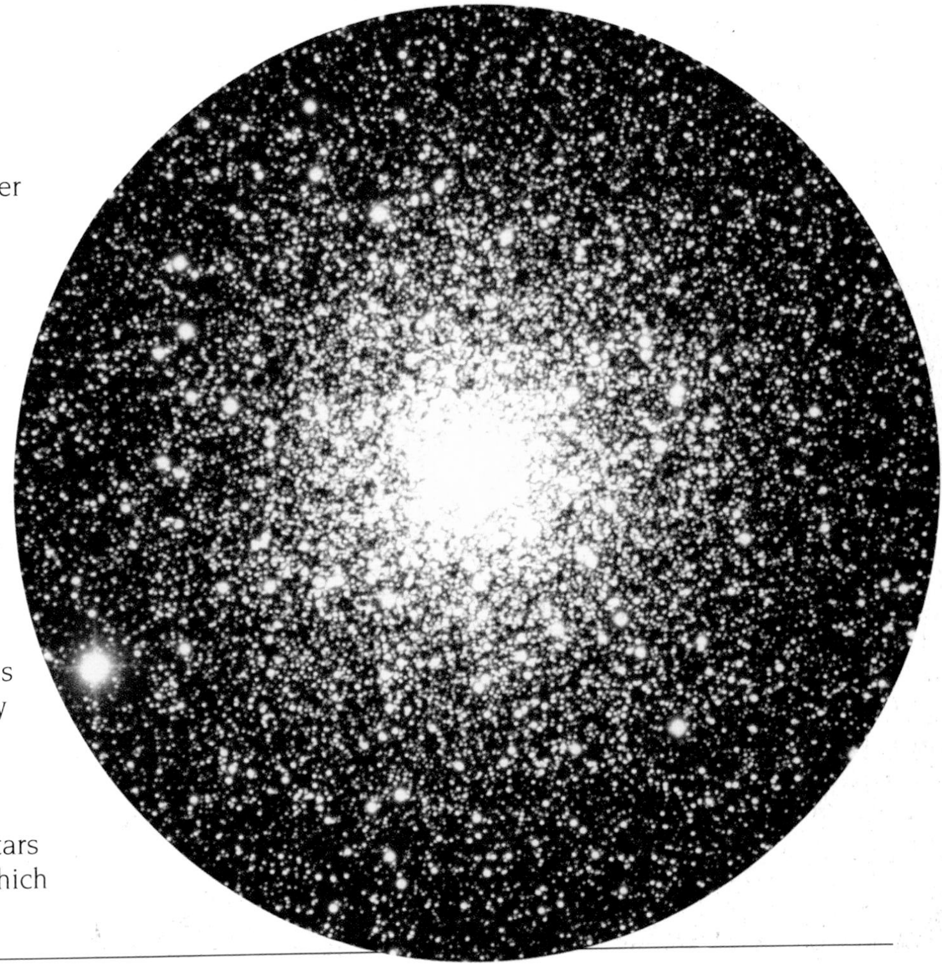

Star clusters

After a while, the gas around a new star cluster disperses into space, so most open star clusters do not have nebulas around them. The stars in an open cluster may become separated. Many of the stars we see in the sky are no longer clustered together.

A star cluster to look out for is the Pleiades, or Seven Sisters, in the constellation Taurus. You can see it with the naked eye. This cluster formed 50 million years ago – more recently than the dinosaurs died out on Earth. The Pleiades have moved away from the cloud where they were born and have ploughed into another one.

As well as open clusters, there are star clusters of a different kind, known as globular clusters. Shaped like balls, they have hundreds of thousands of stars crammed into a small region. All the globular clusters in our own galaxy, the Milky Way, are very old. Many contain stars that formed 10,000 million years ago, which makes them twice as old as our Sun.

ISLANDS OF STARS

On a dark night you might be able to spot an oval-shaped misty patch in the constellation Andromeda. Telescopes reveal that this smudge of light is a spiral galaxy. The Andromeda Galaxy is the nearest large galaxy to our own – 2.5 million light years away.

There are countless galaxies scattered through the Universe. Galaxies are families of stars. Large galaxies have many billions of stars in them. But hardly any stars exist outside galaxies. The Sun belongs to our own galaxy, the Milky Way.

 **key words**

- black hole
- elliptical
- irregular
- quasar
- radio waves
- spiral

Shapes and sizes

Galaxies come in a wide range of sizes. Some dwarf galaxies are only 2000 light years across while the largest giant galaxies extend for more than 500,000 light years.

▲ This image of a spiral galaxy was made by combining several pictures taken by the Hubble Space Telescope. As in most spiral galaxies, the central region contains mostly older, yellow and red stars, while in the outer spiral arms there are younger, blue stars.

About 80 per cent of all galaxies, including both the largest and some of the smallest, are elliptical. They are the shape of a squashed ball. Most of the others are spiral galaxies, with arms that wind outwards from a bulge or bar of stars at the centre. A few fit into neither category so are described as 'irregular'.

Elliptical galaxies contain very little gas and dust. Hardly any new stars are forming in them. Spiral galaxies are disc-shaped with a bulge in the middle. They usually have clouds of dust and gas in the disc where new stars are still being born.

Many galaxies, perhaps all larger ones, have a huge black hole at the centre. Like the black hole that forms when a large star explodes, the one at the centre of a galaxy is so dense, with such strong gravity, that not even light can escape from it. It may have as much mass as thousands or even millions of Suns.

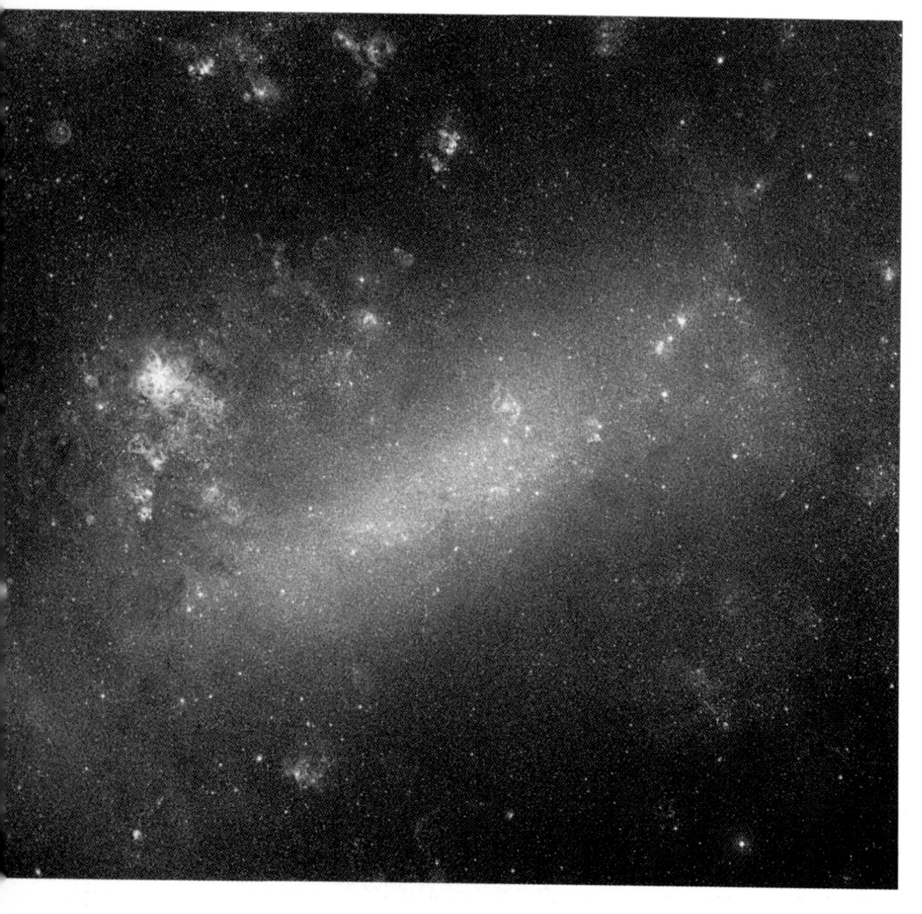

◀ The Large Magellanic Cloud. This small irregular galaxy is a near neighbour, only 170,000 light years away. It is easily visible to the naked eye in the southern constellation Dorado.

Active galaxies

In a few galaxies, called 'active galaxies', the black hole at the centre is dragging in disintegrated stars and gas from a great swirling disc of material around it. So much material falls in that enormous amounts of energy are given off. The galaxy's central region is just a few light years across, but it can be as bright as 100 ordinary galaxies.

These bright point-like sources of light are visible even when they are billions of light years away and the rest of the galaxy is too faint to be seen. They are called quasars – short for 'quasi-stellar radio sources'. They got their name because the first ones to be discovered appeared to be like stars, but emitted powerful radio waves. The most distant objects visible in the Universe are quasars.

The black hole in an active galaxy fires out two opposing jets of particles travelling at close to the speed of light. Some jets give out light but mostly they are detected by radio telescopes. The jets fan out into huge blobs emitting radio waves.

▲ Here, two galaxies are colliding. As a result their shapes have been distorted and the shock blasting through their gas clouds has caused a burst of new stars to form.

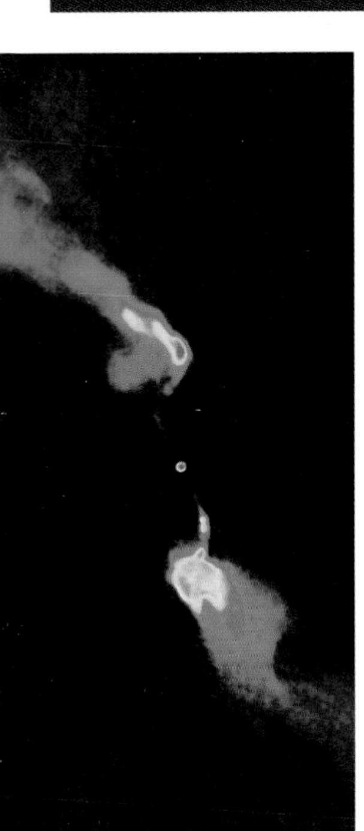

◀ This colour-coded map made by a radio telescope shows two huge lobes of radio-emitting gas on either side of a galaxy called Hydra A. Active galaxies of this kind are called radio galaxies.

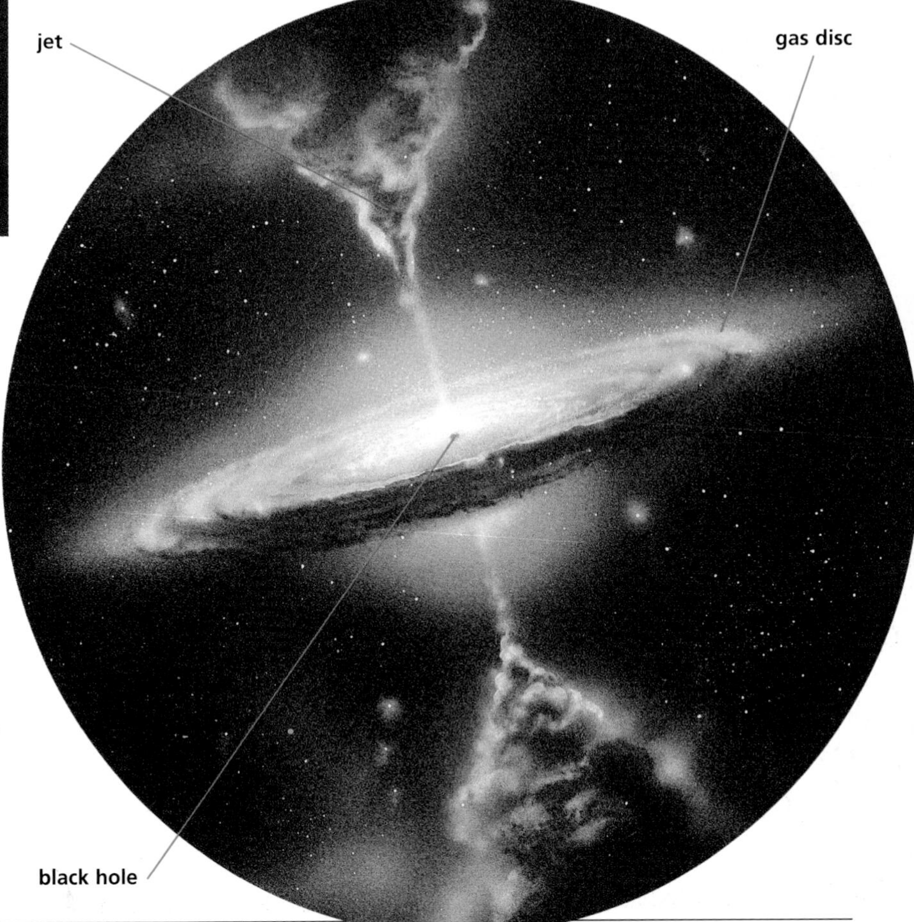

▼ An artist's idea of how the centre of an active galaxy may look. A disc of hot gas swirls around the black hole at the centre. As it falls into the black hole, immense amounts of energy are given out.

OUR GALAXY

The light from billions of distant stars makes a belt of pearly light stretching all the way around the sky. We call it the Milky Way.

The Milky Way is our view of the galaxy we inhabit. It is usually called the Galaxy (with a capital G) or the Milky Way Galaxy. We are about two-thirds of the way out from the centre of a large spiral galaxy.

Most of the 100,000 million stars in the Galaxy are concentrated into a disc with a bulge at the centre. Because we ourselves are inside the disc, we see most stars in a band around us – the Milky Way.

The invisible galaxy

All the stars travel in their own orbits around the centre of the Galaxy. Their speeds show that they are being pulled by the gravity of material that we cannot see, as well as by the other stars and nebulas. No one is sure what the mysterious dark matter is made of, but there seems to be 10 times more dark matter in the Galaxy than stars. A dark halo around the Galaxy could be seven times larger than the disc of stars.

The centre of the Galaxy is hidden from us by thick, dusty clouds, but infrared radiation and radio waves get through. Energy as great as the output of 80 million Suns is pouring from a region smaller than the Solar System. It is thought to come from gas falling into a black hole millions of times more massive than the Sun.

THE MILKY WAY GALAXY
Diameter: 100,000 light years
Distance of Sun from centre: 28,000 light years
Time for Sun to orbit centre: 240 million years
Thickness of disc: 2000 light years
Thickness of central bulge: 10,000 light years
Number of stars: 200 billion
Total mass: 1 million million Suns

▼ Looking towards the centre of our Milky Way. The stars are packed more closely, but many are hidden from us behind dusty clouds.

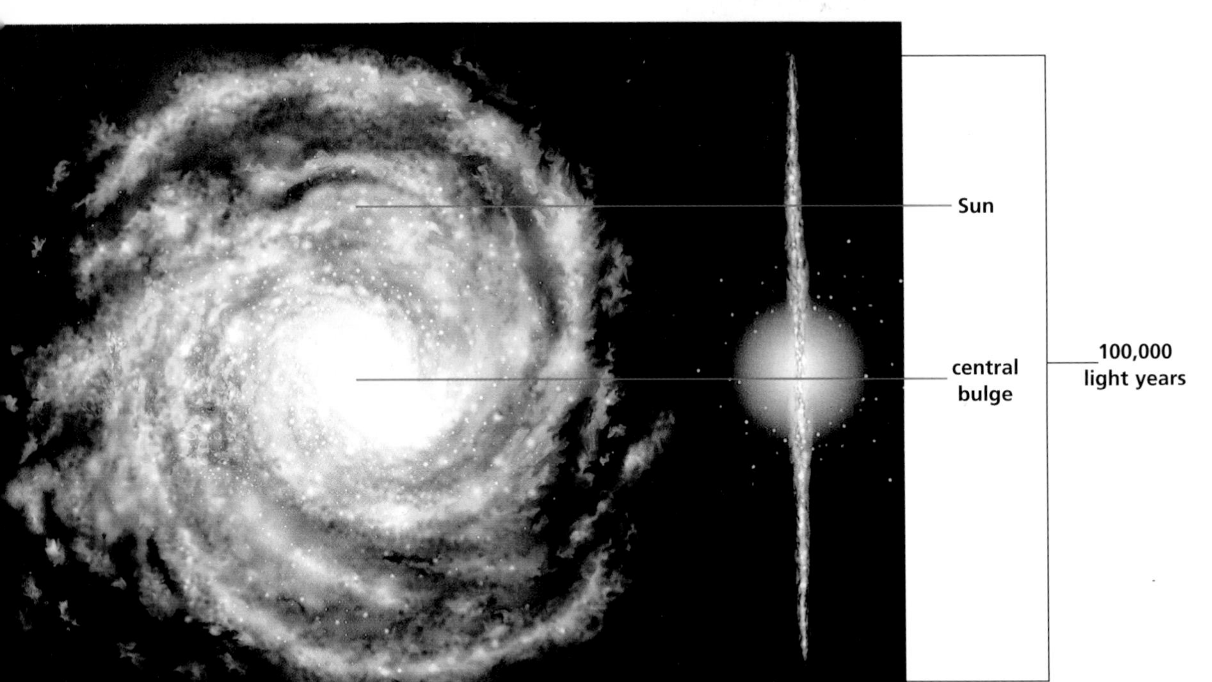

◀ Plans of our Galaxy. Looked at face on, arms spiral outwards from the central bulge. Looked at from the side, the arms create a thin disc shape around the central bulge.

key words
- black hole
- gravity
- infrared

SPACE, TIME AND EVERYTHING

There are about 100,000 million galaxies in the Universe. But they have not always been there. By measuring the motion of galaxies, astronomers have found that the Universe is expanding. Space itself is getting bigger. From the rate of expansion, astronomers think that everything began about 15,000 million years ago, when our visible Universe was concentrated at one point. In a gigantic burst of energy, called the 'Big Bang', our Universe came into being and began to expand.

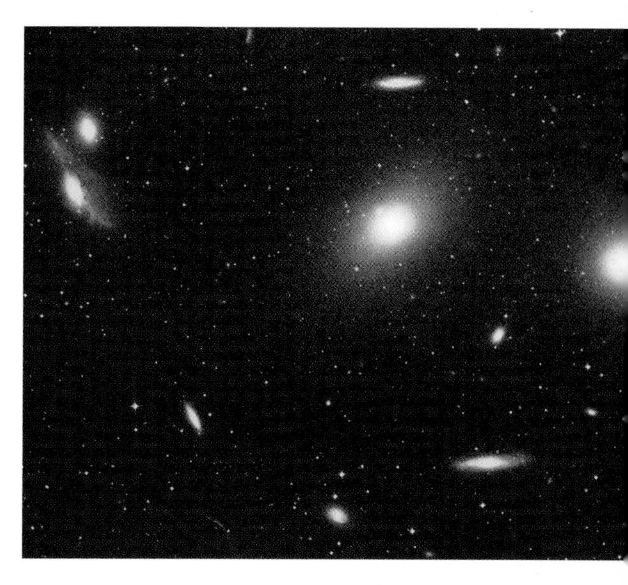

▲ The Virgo cluster of galaxies. These galaxies are about 50 million light years away. The Virgo cluster is one of the nearest to the group of galaxies that includes the Milky Way.

key words

- Big Bang
- gravity
- lens

At the very beginning, the Universe was unimaginably hot and was mainly energy. As it expanded, the Universe cooled down. Matter came into being in the form of the gases hydrogen and helium.

By 1000 million years after the Big Bang, huge gas clouds were starting to pull together under the action of gravity. The first stars were formed in clumps, like large clusters or small galaxies. Clumps merged together to make larger galaxies.

Astronomers can find out what happened long ago in the Universe by looking at very distant galaxies. Even travelling at 300,000 kilometres per second, their light takes billions of years to reach us. This means we see them as they were billions of years ago, as if we were looking back in time.

the Universe more than 10 billion light years across

the Milky Way about 100,000 light years across

the Solar System including the comet cloud, about 0.1 light year across

▲ The scale of the Universe. Each of these pictures is many times larger across than the previous one.

▶ This picture is what the Hubble Space Telescope recorded by looking at a tiny patch of sky for a total of 10 hours. Many of the small blotches are galaxies between 12,000 million and 14,000 million light years away. We see them as they were soon after galaxies first formed in the Universe, because their light has taken so long to reach us.

EDWIN HUBBLE

The US scientist Edwin Hubble (1889–1953) made some of the most important astronomical discoveries of the 20th century. He was the first astronomer to realize that some 'nebulas' in the sky are really galaxies beyond the Milky Way. Hubble measured the speeds and distances of some galaxies and discovered that the farthest galaxies are travelling fastest. This way, he showed that the Universe is expanding. Hubble also invented the system of putting galaxies into categories by their shape. Astronomers still use this system. The Hubble Space Telescope was named in his honour.

Gravity and the Universe

Like stars, galaxies are found in clusters. Clusters stay together because the galaxies are attracted to each other by gravity. Even clusters group together. Over vast expanses of space, they are gathered in strands and walls around empty regions, rather like foamy bubbles.

The gravity of a galaxy cluster is so great, it can even bend the path of a beam of light travelling through it. A cluster can distort and magnify the light from more distant galaxies, acting like a lens.

Gravity is slowing down the expansion of the Universe because the galaxies all pull on each other. But observations of distant galaxies show that a mysterious force called 'dark energy' is acting against gravity. This means that the Universe will probably go on expanding for ever. So far, no one is sure why this is happening.

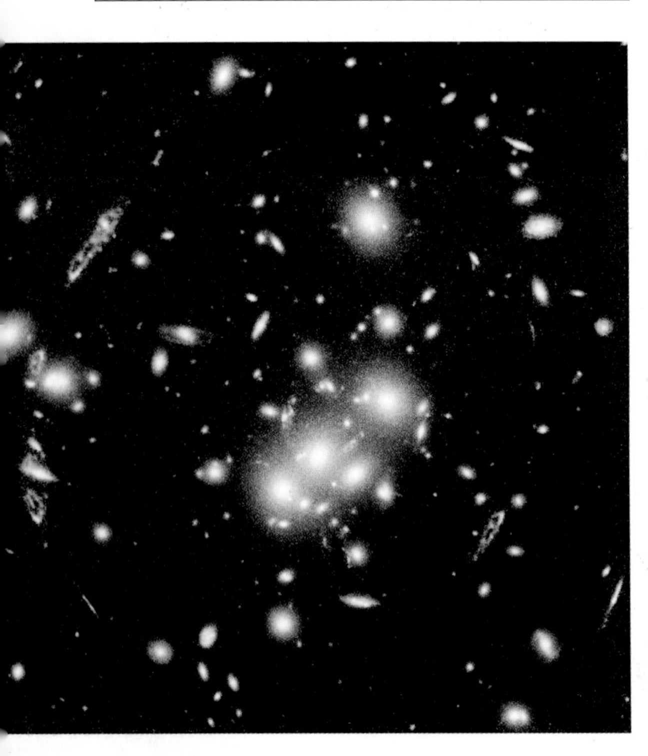

◀ The gravity of a galaxy cluster acting like a lens. The blue objects are all distorted and magnified images of the same galaxy. These multiple images are produced by the powerful gravity of the cluster of galaxies, that look yellowish.

IS THERE LIFE OUT THERE?

Story writers have dreamed up an incredible variety of fearsome creatures inhabiting other worlds in space. So far, though, scientists have found no evidence for life of any kind beyond the Earth.

Earth seems to be a special place for life. There is plenty of liquid water, and living things can get the energy they need from the warm sunlight, or from the heat inside the Earth.

We are now sure that none of the other planets in the Solar System have large plants or animals. Mars, the planet most like the Earth, is one place that might have microscopic life. In the past, Mars was warmer and wetter than it is now. If life started and died out, spacecraft or human explorers might one day find fossils on Mars.

key words
- intelligent life
- radio waves

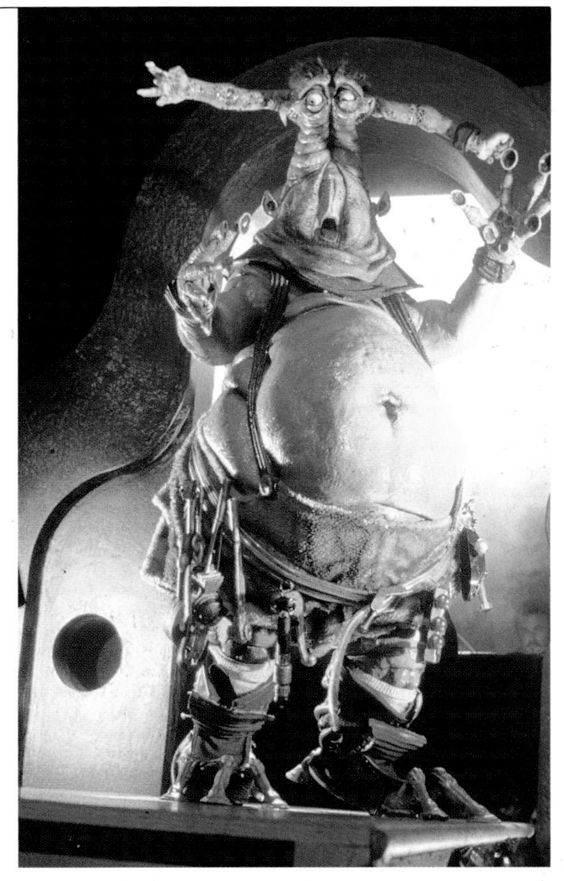

▶ Writers and artists have imagined all kinds of strange alien life, but no one knows whether creatures like this could exist somewhere in the Universe.

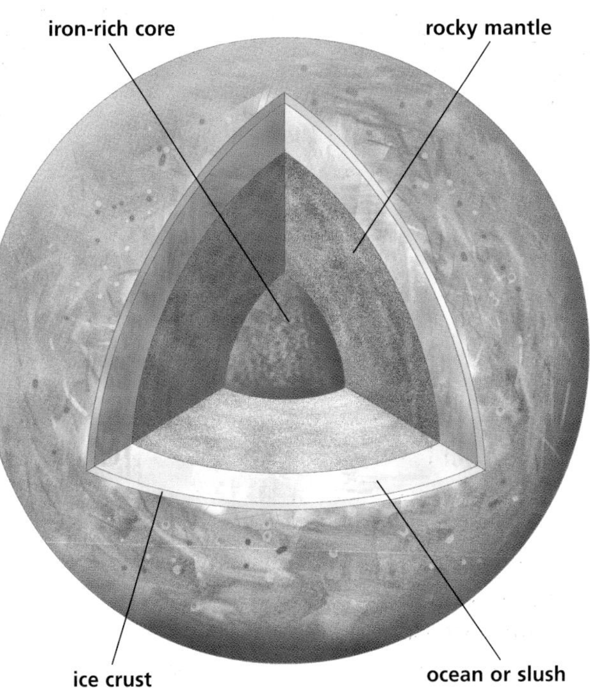

◀ Jupiter's moon Europa could possibly have life. There is probably liquid water under its icy crust. The ice melts because it is stirred around by Jupiter's strong gravity. If there is water, there might be life.

Hunting for extraterrestrials

The Universe is so large, that many people think there must be life of some kind on other planets somewhere. But intelligent life could be very special. We humans might be unique.

Astronomers hope in the future to build telescopes in space to look for telltale signs of life in the atmospheres of planets around nearby stars. Meanwhile, there are projects using large radio telescopes to search for unnatural radio signals from space. Alien radio astronomers up to about 50 light years away could pick up radio signals generated by humans on Earth.

Some people claim that aliens have already visited Earth, but no evidence has yet convinced scientists. There are a whole variety of natural and human explanations for sightings of Unidentified Flying Objects (UFOs).

▶ Millions of people around the world have used their home computers to help in the search for aliens. They sift through huge amounts of data from radio telescopes, looking for artificial signals. The project is called SETI@home. 'SETI' stands for 'Search for Extraterrestrial Intelligence'.

Glossary

The glossary gives simple explanations of difficult or specialist words that readers might be unfamiliar with. Words in *italic* have their own glossary entry.

asteroid A piece of rock or ice that *orbits* the Sun like a tiny *planet*.

atmosphere The layer of gas around a *planet*.

aurora A display of glowing colours seen in the night sky, sometimes called the Northern Lights or the Southern Lights.

Big Bang A theory about the beginning of the *Universe* that says that it exploded from something incredibly tiny and hot and has been expanding ever since.

binary stars A pair of *stars* in *orbit* around each other.

black hole A region in space that has such a strong gravitational pull that no light or matter can escape from it.

comet An object with a bright tail of light, which *orbits* the Sun.

constellation A named area of the night sky, usually centred around a familiar pattern of *stars*.

eclipse The blocking of the Sun's light when the Moon comes between the Earth and the Sun (solar eclipse) or the blocking of the Moon's light when the Earth comes between the Moon and the Sun (lunar eclipse).

ecliptic The Sun's path around the sky, which it takes one year to complete.

elliptical Shaped like an ellipse, which is a curved shape like a squashed or elongated circle.

galaxy A family of millions or billions of *stars*, often containing great amounts of dust and gas.

gravity The force that attracts two objects. Earth's gravity keeps everything on Earth from floating out into space.

light year The distance that light travels in one year (about 9.5 million million kilometres).

meteor A bright trail in the night sky created when a grain of dust or a rock fragment from space burns up in the *atmosphere*; meteors are sometimes called shooting stars.

meteorite A piece of rock or metal from space that lands on the surface of the Earth or another *planet*.

meteoroid Any natural object *orbiting* the Sun with a size in the range from a grain of dust to about 100 metres across.

Milky Way The *galaxy* to which the *Solar System* belongs.

moon A body *orbiting* a *planet*.

neutron star A collapsed *star* in which most of the mass (weight) of the star packs down into a ball about 10 km across.

nuclear energy Energy released when the nuclei of atoms collide.

orbit The path that one body takes around another, especially the path taken by something moving round a planet or other body in space.

phase The proportion of the face of the Moon, or a *planet*, that is visible because it is lit by sunlight.

planet A body in space that is not massive enough to generate *nuclear energy* and become a *star*.

radar A navigation system that uses radio waves to detect the presence of an object at a distance.

radiation Energy that can travel through empty space at the speed of light (300,000 kilometres per second). Infrared, radio waves, ultraviolet and X-rays are all kinds of radiation.

red giant An old *star* that has increased greatly in size and is reaching the end of its life. Red giants have a relatively cool surface that glows red.

satellite A small object in *orbit* around a larger one; *moons* are natural satellites.

Solar System The Sun and the family of *planets* and other objects that *orbit* around it.

star A large ball of hot, glowing gas that shines with its own light because it is generating *nuclear energy* inside. The Sun is an example of a star.

Universe Everything that exists, including the Earth, all its creatures and the heavenly bodies.

white dwarf An old collapsed *star* that has run out of nuclear fuel at its centre and is in the process of dying. White dwarfs are thought to be the contracted cores of *red giants*.

INDEX

Page numbers in **bold** mean that this is where you will find the most information on that subject. If both a heading and a page number are in bold, there is an article with that title. A page number in *italic* means that there is a picture of that subject. There may also be other information about the subject on the same page.

Acknowledgements

Key
t = top; c = centre; b = bottom; r = right; l = left; back = background; fore = foreground.

Artwork
Baum, Julian: 6 tl; 15 t; 17 b; 18 tl; 19 tl; 20 tl; 22 tl; 24 tl; 26 tl; 28 tl; 29 tl; 31 b; 42 b. **D'Achille, Gino**: 5 br; 10 bl; 28 cr; 32 br; 44 c. **Hardy, David**: 8 tr; 9 b; 32 b; 34 b. **Jakeway, Rob**: 10 tr; 11 t; 18 tr; 19 tr; 21 t; 23 c; 26 b; 27 t; 41 b; 43 tl, b. **Parsley, Helen**: 5 cr. **Rawlings, Pat**: 30 tr. **Saunders, Mike**: 6 b; 8 b; 10–11 c; 12 b; 15 b; 17 bl; 24 cr; 28 tr; 34 tr; 36 b; 45 b. **Sneddon, James**: 16 c. **Stewart, Roger**: 13 r; 30 bl; 45 bl. **Visscher, Peter**: 4 tl; 8 tl; 10 tl; 12 tl; 14 tl; 17 tl; 30 tl; 31 tl; 32 tl; 33 tl; 38 tl; 42 tl; 45 tl.

Photos
The publishers would like to thank the following for permission to use their photographs.

(c) Anglo-Australian Observatory: 36 tr (Photograph by David Malin); 37 tr (Photograph by David Malin); 38 bl (Royal Observatory, Edinburgh); 39 t (Royal Observatory, Edinburgh); 39 b (Photograph by David Malin); 40 b (Royal Observatory, Edinburgh); 41 tl (Photograph by David Malin); 42 c (Photograph by David Malin); 43 tr (Royal Observatory, Edinburgh).

ESO: 37 br; 40 tr.

Espenak, Fred (Photograph (c)1999 by Fred Espenak, www.MrEclipse.com): 4 bl.

Evans, Dr Nigel: 33 tr.

Kobal: 45 tr (Paramount).

Mitton, Jacqueline: 5 bl; 7 br; 12 tr (Kitt Peak Observatory); 16 tr; 22 tr; 22 b (NASA/HST); 24 ct (Hubble Space Telescope Comet Team/NASA); 27 bl (NASA/JPL); 28 br (NASA/JPL); 30 c (NASA/HST); 30 br (NASA, Pat Rawlings); 41 bl (Gregory B. Taylor, National Radio Astronomy Observatory and University of California, L.A.).

NASA: 6 tr (IMP Team, JPL); 7 tr; 6 cr (NASA/CXC/SO); 14 tr (JSC); 18 bl; 19 c; 23 tr; 23 br (JPL); 24 b; 25 tl, cl, cb, ct; 26 tr (R.Beebe (NMSU)); 28 bl (E. Karkoschka (LPL)); 29 tr (JPL); 29 bl (ESA); 29 br; 31 tr (Johns Hopkins University Applied Physics Laboratory); 35 t (A. Dupree (CfA)); 35 b (NASA/HST, J. Morse/K. Davidson); 37 tl [Hubble Heritage Team (AURA/ STScI/ NASA)]; 36 tl [Hubble Heritage Team (AURA/ STScI/ NASA)]; 44 tr (R. Williams); 44 bl (W. Colley, Princeton University).

Photodisc: 14 b; 16 tl; 19 br; 20 bl; 27 br; 32 tl; 33 b; 40 tl.

PPARC: 17 tr.
Science Photo Library: 4 tr (Martin Bond); 16 b (Frank Zullo); 20 cr ((c) W. T. Sullivan III); 21 r (Pekka Parviainen); 32 tr (Tony and Daphne Hallas); 33 cr (David Parker); 38 tr (Andrew Fruchter, STSci).

SETI: 45 b.

Suetterlin, Dr Peter: 13 cl (DOT Team, SIU).